# FOUL DEEDS & SUSPICIOUS DEATHS AROUND SOUTHEND-ON-SEA

# TRUE CRIME FROM WHARNCLIFFE

*Foul Deeds and Suspicious Deaths Series*

Barking, Dagenham & Chadwell Heath
Barnsley
Bath
Bedford
Birmingham
Black Country
Blackburn and Hyndburn
Bolton
Bradford
Brighton
Bristol
Cambridge
Carlisle
Chesterfield
Colchester
Coventry
Croydon
Derby
Durham
Ealing
Folkestone and Dover
Grimsby
Guernsey
Guilford
Halifax
Hampstead, Holborn and St Pancras
Huddersfield
Hull

Leeds
Leicester
Lewisham and Deptford
Liverpool
London's East End
London's West End
Manchester
Mansfield
More Foul Deeds Birmingham
More Foul Deeds Chesterfield
More Foul Deeds Wakefield
Newcastle
Newport
Norfolk
Northampton
Nottingham
Oxfordshire
Pontefract and Castleford
Portsmouth
Rotherham
Scunthorpe
Southend-on-Sea
Staffordshire and The Potteries
Stratford and South Warwickshire
Tees
Warwickshire
Wigan
York

# OTHER TRUE CRIME BOOKS FROM WHARNCLIFFE

A-Z Yorkshire Murder
Black Barnsley
Brighton Crime and Vice 1800-2000
Durham Executions
Essex Murders
Executions & Hangings in Newcastle
    and Morpeth
Norfolk Mayhem and Murder

Norwich Murders
Strangeways Hanged
The A-Z of London Murders
Unsolved Murders in Victorian and
    Edwardian London
Unsolved Norfolk Murders
Unsolved Yorkshire Murders
Yorkshire's Murderous Women

Please contact us via any of the methods below for more information or a catalogue.

## WHARNCLIFFE BOOKS

47 Church Street – Barnsley – South Yorkshire – S70 2AS
Tel: 01226 734555 – 734222 Fax: 01226 – 734438
E-mail: enquiries@pen-and-sword.co.uk
Website: www.wharncliffebooks.co.uk

## Foul Deeds and Suspicious Deaths Around

# SOUTHEND-ON-SEA

Dee Gordon

**Wharncliffe Books**

First published in Great Britain in 2007
and reprinted in 2012, 2020, 2021 and 2022 by
**Wharncliffe Books**
*an imprint of*
**Pen & Sword Books Ltd**
**47 Church Street**
**Barnsley**
**South Yorkshire**
**S70 2AS**

Copyright © Dee Gordon 2007, 2012, 2020, 2021, 2022

**ISBN 978 18456 304 78**

A CIP catalogue record for this book is
available from the British Library

Typeset in Plantin and ITC Benguiat by Mousemat Design Limited

Printed and bound in the UK on FSC accredited paper by
4edge Ltd, Essex, SS5 4AD

*Pen & Sword Books Ltd incorporates the imprints of*
Pen & Sword Aviation, Pen & Sword Family History, Pen & Sword Maritime,
Pen & Sword Military, Pen & Sword Discovery, Pen & Sword Politics,
Pen & Sword Atlas, Pen & Sword Archaeology, Wharncliffe Local History,
Wharncliffe True Crime, Wharncliffe Transport, Pen & Sword Select,
Pen & Sword Military Classics, Leo Cooper, The Praetorian Press,
Claymore Press, Remember When, Seaforth Publishing and Frontline Publishing

*For a complete list of Pen & Sword titles please contact*
PEN & SWORD BOOKS LIMITED
47 Church Street, Barnsley, South Yorkshire, S70 2AS, England.
E-mail: enquiries@pen-and-sword.co.uk
Website: www.pen-and-sword.co.uk

# Contents

# Acknowledgements

Thanks to Becky Latchford and Martyn Lockwood from the Essex Police Museum, Jenny Butler and Vanda Jeffrey from Essex Record Office, Pat Reynolds at Surrey Heritage, Dot Bedenham at Chelmsford Museum and everyone at the Rural Life Museum, Southend Central Library, and the British Newspaper Library at Colindale, London. Not forgetting Mark Kimber, Pat Stone at Southend University Hospital, Peter Owen www.flickr.com and Richard Platt, writer, www.smuggling.co.uk for their help with photographs, Donna Lowe for her help with research, Judith Williams for her search tips, and Triple Knot www.pierrepoint.co.uk.

Southend rising from the mud in the nineteenth century. (*Author's Collection*)

# Introduction

Southend-on-Sea. A name that conjures up the stereotypical British seaside, complete with buckets and spades, brash amusement arcades, jellied eels – and the longest pier in the world. Or a name that suggests a peaceful retirement, bearing in mind the 2005/6 Government think-tank that noted Southend-on-Sea as one of the safest towns in England and Wales. Certainly at first glance the town offers commuting heaven, luxury (always luxury) seafront apartments, surrounded by historic villages, full of individual character. Dig a little deeper, however, and a darker side is revealed. As it always will be, whatever the location and regardless of how peaceful and appealing the setting might seem: just ask Miss Marple.

So this book is designed to dish some ancient dirt, and remind the reader – resident or otherwise – that tempers have always flared, feelings have often run high, and extremely nasty crimes were committed long before the days of road-rage or drug-related violence. Foul deeds motivated by greed, jealousy and revenge are still with us. Similarly, murder motivated by religious belief – sharing a common ground with racism – is not a recent phenomenon. There is evidence of such crimes hundreds of years ago in the Southend area.

Something to bear in mind is that Southend-on-Sea, as such, did not exist until late in the eighteenth century, having started life as the 'south end' of Prittlewell. By 1725 the coastline from Shoeburyness to Hadleigh was sown with oyster layings and dwellings were needed for workers in this industry; perhaps the first to be erected were in Pleasant Row, near the now-famous Kursaal. The area's population grew from a few hundred in 1801 to nearly 12,000 in 1891, following the railway boom of the 1850s, and this figure had doubled again by 1901. This book is centred on Southend-on-Sea, now the largest town in Essex,

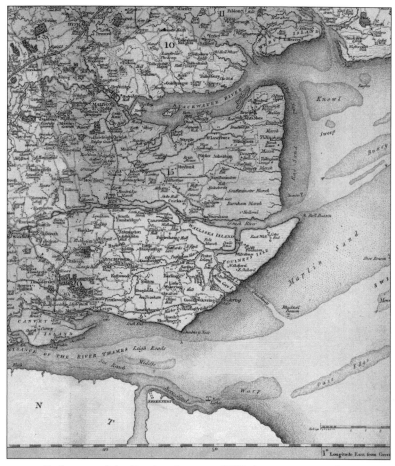

Early map of the Southend area, *c.* 1808. (*Peter Owen Collection*)

but also covers the surrounding area. Villages such as Canewdon and Paglesham are included, as are former villages that are now virtually suburbs of Southend, such as Leigh-on-Sea and Shoeburyness. A few cases from nearby Laindon and Rayleigh have also been included because of their notoriety.

The crimes singled out for attention in the pages that follow are intended not to glorify crime itself but to consider why such things happened and to examine how differently they have been dealt with over the centuries. Although the majority date from after 1800, this does not mean that crime is on the increase, only that the reporting of crime has greatly expanded since the advent of the newspaper.

# CHAPTER 1

# Medieval Crimes

Anyone attempting to track down crimes from as far back as the thirteenth and fourteenth centuries meets a frustrating combination of legend, Chinese whispers and unreliable translations from French chroniclers such as Jean Froissart. Only among the aristocracy are such crimes recorded in any detail, not because they were more criminally inclined than the peasants (or working classes) – far from it – but because the misdemeanours of the latter went mainly unrecorded for posterity unless they impacted on their rulers and masters. Tracking individual crimes any further back is virtually impossible as the area was so sparsely populated, and the foul deeds that are on record are in respect of local battles – of Benfleet, say, or Ashingdon.

The first person whose foul deeds are on record in the Southend area is Sir Richard de Southchurch, known as Richard the Extortioner (*c*. 1227–94). The Sheriff of Essex and the King's Steward of the Liberty of Rochford, he held a 900-acre manor encompassing Southchurch, Prittlewell, Leigh, Shopland, North Shoebury, Sutton and Rayleigh. At least some of his wealth, however, seems to have resulted from his abuse of his position as sheriff. This role required him to provide military stores for the King's forces when they were in Essex, and he did indeed requisition large quantities of wheat, oats, corn, oxen, cattle, cheese and hams in the name of King Henry III. Added to this list were great quantities of chickens to feed the army's wounded, plus 400 eggs for poultices, linen and rags for bandages, and pickaxes and spades to break down the walls of London, held in 1267 by rebel supporters of Simon de Montfort. One interesting acquisition made during this struggle was of eight cocks which Sir Richard claimed would have fire tied to their feet and then be sent flying over London to burn the city. Not only did large quantities of such stores end up at his house in Southchurch, but Sir Richard also raised cash from the Exchequer by billing them for hundreds of marks for supplies that had cost him nothing. He was something of a Robin Hood in reverse. Regarded as an impudent and ingenious rascal, he is also alleged to have arrested innocent men and demanded that they pay for their release; this was not something that could easily be achieved without violence.

After the accession of Edward I in 1272 the men of Rochford Hundred brought a long list of charges against Sir Richard for his abuse of his position as a royal official during the troubled years following the breakdown of Henry III's government. Additional charges included appointing bailiffs to commit acts of extortion on his behalf, demanding excessive fines and refusing bail after taking the agreed funds. In 1279 he was charged with taking a hart without the King's authority, but it seems he somehow managed to evade punishment even though at that time the penalty for poaching deer or boar in Rayleigh, Rochford and Hadleigh forests was to be blinded. He did, however, serve some time in London's Fleet prison in 1285, and forfeited his manors at Eastwood and Hatfield Peverel to the King, so perhaps he did not escape scot-free. It would be good to think so.

★★★

A nastier turn of events took place half a century later in the unlikely environs of Prittlewell Priory – or perhaps not so unlikely given the 1170 martyrdom of Thomas Becket in Canterbury Cathedral. William de Auvergnat, a monk from Lewes, was appointed Prior in 1311 but by 1314 had managed to embroil himself in some complex legal and financial difficulties including accusations of 'incontinency [unrestrained behaviour, often sexual] whilst in London'. As a result he was removed from office but he refused to accept this decision, regarding it as unfair.

In protest, Prior William invaded Prittlewell Priory with an armed mob and seized it, expelling the monks, breaking chests, appropriating the monuments and the common seal, damaging the convent's goods and committing other violent and inappropriate excesses. Realising his mistake, he then offered to renounce his rights before being judged. This offer was acceptable, both to the Prior and the King, but William, still angry, again forcibly entered the Priory, trying the King's patience. The King ordered his arrest, along with his supporters, but William refused to give up the struggle and was reinstalled, ejected and reinstalled again until in 1321 the Prior of Lewes determined to settle the matter once and for all.

While William was celebrating mass at the high altar, it seems that an armed force sent by the Prior of Lewes arrived to take possession of the Priory. William and his monks were outnumbered and the bloody battle that ensued ended with William and three of his monks being badly wounded. All were bound hand and foot and thrown into a cart to be carried off to

Interior of Prittlewell Priory. (*Author's Collection*)

Prittlewell Priory in 2007. (*Author*)

Lewes, along with the Priory's common seal. Soon afterwards William died, no doubt because of the severe head wound he had received. It is not known whether any charges of manslaughter were brought, but it seems unlikely. Ironically, if William had survived he would probably have been restored to his coveted position as Prior of Prittlewell because of this last unauthorised attack.

*★★★*

From Sir Richard and Prior William we move on to the insurrection that put peasants into recorded history: the Peasants' Revolt of 1381, which proved to be an important milestone on the road to freedom. The labour shortage caused by the Black Death of 1348–9 is thought to have given the peasants some bargaining power, and they were not afraid to use it. Following the imposition of a series of taxes intended to raise money to pay for the wars with France and to cover administrative shortfalls in the economy, the government attempted to collect a further groat (about 2p) from every poor person over 15 years of age. Commissioners were appointed to travel to various parts of Essex to compel collection of the tax. The inhabitants of Fobbing, Corringham and Stanford-le-Hope were summoned to Brentwood to settle their 'debt' but they arrived in hostile mood and refused to make any further payments. The Fobbing fishermen had been excused an earlier tax because of their poverty, but this time they resorted to threats of violence against the commissioner Thomas Bampton and his sergeants, driving them back to London. Fearful of the possible consequences of their actions, the villagers hid for a while in the woods, before hunger eventually drove them back home. Hailed as heroes, they soon began a campaign to rouse other villagers.

A few days later the Chief Justice of the King's Bench had another try at collecting the tax at Brentwood but a great crowd of protesters turned up and in the subsequent brawl six men (three from each faction) were killed. The violence escalated and John Ewell, an Essex officer (of property law), was beheaded at Langdon Hills and his head paraded on a lance.

It took just a week for more than 20,000 men from Essex and Kent to gather and begin their march on London, setting out on

Southchurch Hall, 2007. (*Author*)

11 June. The sheriff's manor house and the abbey at Coggeshall were looted. The manors of Milton and Barn Hall (at Downham) were similarly ransacked, as were those of Wakering Hall and Paglesham. Southchurch Hall was allegedly ransacked and burned, although no evidence survives other than references to the destruction of court rolls (presumably kept there). Hadleigh Mill was attacked and the King's books there were apparently seized. It seems these actions were part of an attempt by the marauding peasants to destroy the records of official precedents for duties and fines imposed on labourers.

Local men involved included John Messenger at Prittlewell, who was later indicted as a common disturber of the peace and supporter of malefactors in the rising. Others were from Shoebury (including John Hurt and John Syrat), Rochford (including John Glasiere), Prittlewell (Thomas Walston), Rayleigh (Henry Trecche), Benfleet (Thomas Spragge), Leigh (Thomas Treche), Hadleigh (William Bocher, Richard Bell, John Symond, John atte Marsh), Wakering (John Buck), Paglesham (Peter White), Stambridge and Canewdon. Ralph Spicer was among those hanged for taking part in the rebellion, but he was one of the luckier ones, bearing in mind that the revolt followed the introduction of the ultimate punishment: being hanged, drawn and quartered.

When they finally reached London, the men demanded the abolition of serfdom but the very young King Richard II reneged on his initial agreement to give them 'all you seek', instead threatening even worse treatment. Opposition to yet another tax had turned into bloody armed resistance against the King. Predictably, the peasants' ill-defended encampment at Rettendon was attacked by the King's army and at least 500 local rebels were killed. An amnesty of sorts followed, with the sparing of 247 men whose names appeared on a death list, but many had to forfeit possessions. One, Robert Eggot of Corringham, was obliged to surrender his homestead worth 40 shillings.

★★★

Next we find an all-round nasty individual whose name reputedly 'stank in Essex nostrils' because of his own involvement in the slaughter of the oppressed fighting for justice. Blood-lust was seemingly one of his favourite leisure pursuits. John de Holland was Duke of Exeter and Earl of Huntingdon; a half-brother of Richard II, he was also a Knight of the Garter. The rack, that infamous instrument of torture at the Tower of London where Holland was Constable for a year, was not known as the 'Duke of Exeter's daughter' without good reason. Froissart, the French chronicler, portrays him as a violent ruffian.

In 1384 Holland was involved with the cold-blooded murder of a Carmelite friar, who was in his custody prior to an enquiry into some unsavoury allegations. Holland does not seem to have been indicted for this butchery. A year later, he murdered again. This time the victim was the Earl of Stafford's son, one of whose archers had slain one of Holland's esquires following a quarrel. The Earl of Stafford demanded revenge and Holland's lands were seized shortly after. While this could be construed as a possible 'punishment', the lands were restored to him a year later after he had done no more than arrange a church service for the repose of the soul of Stafford's son – or perhaps it was because he had, in the interim, eloped with and seduced John of

Hadleigh Castle. (*Richard Platt Collection*)

Gaunt's daughter, resulting in a hastily arranged marriage. Gaunt's daughter no doubt needed some kind of dowry.

In 1397 Holland came to the Southend area. On the orders of Richard II, he ambushed the King's uncle, Thomas of Woodstock, Duke of Gloucester, the man who had taken control of the government by removing young Richard's friends and advisers. Woodstock was taken to Calais, where he was strangled with knotted towels and his body embalmed and cased in lead. His body was returned by sea to Hadleigh Castle. Legend has it that the coffin was held en route at Leigh-on-Sea, which is the most likely point for it to be off-loaded. From Hadleigh Castle poor old Woodstock was taken further north to Pleshey, where he was finally laid to rest. A version of this murder is chronicled in Shakespeare's *Richard II* without reference to John de Holland, but of course Shakespeare was not averse to omitting 'unsuitable' material or manipulating events to suit his plots.

Two years later the situation for Holland changed and it was his turn to be on the receiving end of a foul deed. Richard II was deposed, and his successor, Henry IV, regarded Holland as a traitor. So Holland fled from Oxford to Hadleigh, the seat of the Earl of Oxford, and from there to Milton Shore, where he tried to escape by sea but was driven back and delayed by bad weather (nothing changes). He seems to have taken refuge in Hamlet Mill (in the area now known as Westcliff-on-Sea) while waiting for conditions to improve. While enjoying dinner there with John Prittlewell he was besieged by local villagers, mostly from Milton Hamlet (now part of Southend). They 'arrested' Holland and took him to Pleshey where he was tortured and torn to pieces by Woodstock's tenants and servants in an act of savage vengeance. He was then beheaded, on the say-so of Woodstock's mother-in-law, the Countess of Hereford, and seemingly not necessarily with Henry's blessing, given that Holland was his brother-in-law. It was generally regarded as a well-deserved fate for a man of such violent character.

# CHAPTER 2

# Murderers, Paedophiles and the Marian Martyrs

## (1500–1699)

Although William the Conqueror banned executions throughout our green and pleasant land, they were brought back after his death in 1087, with hanging becoming the most acceptable form of capital punishment throughout Britain, rather than the earlier, messier, beheading. By the sixteenth century summary justice for minor offences was meted out not by central or local government officials but by constables elected by the parish. These constables were local representatives whose most important duty was probably to raise the 'hue and cry' after a robbery or murder had taken place. The parish constable was below the church warden in the parish hierarchy but he would have carried a staff of office and a pair of handcuffs. For nearly 300 years the constables were the main force in combating crime. The stocks were used to punish drunkards, with lock-ups to detain those awaiting trial in Chelmsford. There are records of such lock-ups in just about all the villages that preceded Southend, from Rettendon for example in the north, to Foulness in the east. The 'crime' of vagrancy was particularly common and by the end of the sixteenth century was punishable with a public flogging (for both men and women), but this was preferable to being branded and sold into slavery, which could have been the punishment had they been born in a different century.

By the seventeenth century some communities had progressed from lock-ups to small gaolhouses: there had reputedly been a gaolhouse in the Shoebury area for hundreds of years by this time, and there was another one in a terrace of three houses near the junction of Downhall and London Roads in Rayleigh. Every hamlet had its own stocks and whipping post for lesser offences. Stocks stood at Parsons Corner, Shoeburyness, and a set of stocks is preserved inside the building formerly used as a lock-up in Canewdon. Whipping as

The lock-up at Bradwell-on-Sea. (*Author's Collection*)

a punishment dates back to Saxon times, with vagrants singled out as victims by Henry VIII with his Whipping Act of 1530. Inside Little Wakering Church is an example of a whipping post, brought here from its original position for safe-keeping.

If the perpetrators of more serious crimes got as far as a court trial, then it was possible for them to be sentenced to death by hanging, a public event once regarded as something of a day out for the family. Records of such events are scarce, but

Samuel Pepys gives a typical account in April 1664, describing how he stood 'upon a wheel of a cart' to get a good view, which cost him a shilling, as a 'comely-looked' man was hanged for robbery, with 'twelve to fourteen thousand people in the street'. The county gaol was originally at Colchester Castle, 30 miles north of Southend, but prison sentences were a rarity until the sixteenth century. The death sentence was common for offences that today seem relatively minor, such as petty theft, although stolen goods were often under-valued (at less than 12*d*) to avoid

Cartoon 'A Room With a View'. (*Author's Collection*)

making it a capital offence. In 1576 it became a legal requirement for each county to have its own house of correction, and the first in Essex seems to be the one recorded at Corringham in 1587.

Records of local 'foul deeds', including murders, committed during this period are frustratingly brief, with no additional trial information accessible even from the National Archives at Kew. Early cases include the alleged murder of a 12-year-old girl, Joan Johnson, in 1559, at 'Cannouden', now Canewdon. The coroner, Thomas Knott, played a vital role in this case, as coroners often did. The accused were yeomen farmers, Elizabeth and [illegible] Heckesford senior of Canewdon. They pleaded not guilty, claiming that young Joan drowned herself, but they were accused of assault and murder. The coroner must have favoured the Heckesfords' version of events, because they were found not guilty.

In a 1592 case before Robert Clarke, Baron of the Exchequer, and Thomas Walmesley, Judge of the Common Pleas or Queen's Bench, Mary Crowche (spelt variously as Crouche), a widow, and Abraham Lynsey, a labourer, both of Paglesham, were indicted for murder after an inquisition held at Paglesham in June before Thomas Drywood, coroner, on the body of Thomas Blakbone of Paglesham, a tailor. It appears that Crowche and Lynsey attacked Blakbone in his house at Paglesham at about 11pm on 18 April, during which attack he was strangled by Crowche, abetted by Lynsey. Another tailor, Ambrose Duckford of Paglesham, was indicted as an accessory, although none of the three seems to have attempted to escape the scene after the murder.

The all-male jury comprised Robert Hodge, John Dyxon, Eustace Kynnett, William Tedym, Thomas Bewley, William Dyxon, Richard Hewes, Richard Eve, Richard Emerson, John Kene, Robert Bonnam, William Smyth, Edward Canwedon (*sic*) and John Reade. Although all the defendants pleaded not guilty, the jury found both Crowche and Lynsey guilty, and Lynsey was subsequently hanged. Crowche was remanded owing to pregnancy, and Duckford was found not guilty. It is interesting to speculate on the circumstances – the eternal triangle, a drunken argument, a violent husband, perhaps – but sadly, we'll never know.

Paglesham in 1592 seems to have been a hotbed of violent crime. On 10 August Thomas Buley, a yeoman, assaulted William Tedymer and struck him with a dagger worth 12*s*. (The value of the weapon was considered a crucial factor when deciding on the sentence.) The attack resulted in a 'thrust upon his back' that left him with a mortal wound 3 inches deep and 1 inch wide. He died early in September, and Buley was indicted for murder 'with malice aforethought'. The trial took place in March 1593 before Sir Thomas Mildmay, Sir Thomas Lucas, Sir John Petre, James Morris, attorney of the Court of Wards, Robert Wroth JP, Francis Barrington JP, and a grand jury. Interestingly, this case is summed up with the words 'at large' – whether Thomas Buley was ever caught remains a tantalising mystery.

One Essex indictment in March 1620 resulted in the hanging of Richard Jackson from Leigh-on-Sea (then Leigh) for an offence still regarded with revulsion. The Justice of the King's Bench at his trial in Chelmsford was Robert Houghton, attended by a serjeant-at-law named variously as Ranulph or Randal Crewe. Jackson, described as a 'husbandman' (farmer), was indicted for the rape of four schoolgirls. The first three, raped in Leigh-on-Sea on 2 February 1619, were Mary Goodladd, aged 10, Rachel Bonner, aged 11, and Liddia Duke, also 11. The fourth victim, Elizabeth Dagnett, aged 12, was raped a year later in the same area, on 10 January 1620. According to the Calendar of Essex Assize Records, Jackson was committed by Edward Butler and Anthony Ware, and the witnesses were named as Sara Saier, William Goodladd and John Syms, with William Bower, Elizabeth Neale and Sara Steele listed as giving evidence. It is interesting that all four schoolgirls were also listed as witnesses. Although Jackson pleaded not guilty, he was found guilty and hanged – by the same judge who had imposed the death sentence on Simon Langfield of Foulness for stealing a cap, a sheet, a pair of hose, a jerkin, a hat, a tablecloth and cash totalling £3 17s.

Hanging was also the penalty imposed on Jonathon Fayers from Thundersley in January 1649 for the murder of Edmund Allum. This record mentions Thomas Mann as the coroner. The jurors believed that Fayers, a glazier, assaulted Allum with 'a sodering iron' (*sic*) worth 6d giving him a mortal bruise on the forepart of his head, whereby he died instantly. The crime took place in December, but the date of execution is not recorded.

One man who escaped execution was Richard Sable, who murdered the Wickford butcher John Osbourne. He was arrested and imprisoned at Colchester Castle, and found guilty at the Chelmsford Assizes on 17 August 1641. However, because he could read he was branded and 'delivered', or in other words released.

## THE MARIAN MARTYRS

In July 1553 Edward VI was succeeded by his elder sister Mary, daughter of Henry VIII. As a result, England was forced to revert to Catholicism, which it had shaken off during Henry's reign – more accurately, during his wooing of Anne Boleyn, when the King fell out with the Pope and established the Protestant Church of England. It seems that, then as now, people were willing to sacrifice their lives for religious doctrine and principles.

A Thundersley man, Thomas Causton, an influential manor holder, is especially remembered for his beliefs and his bravery. His money, esteem and influence carried no weight in such a situation. He was arrested and tried for heresy, as recorded in Foxe's famous *Book of Martyrs*, published in 1563. Causton and his friend Thomas Highbed, along with Causton's servant, were initially arrested for refusing to renounce their Protestant beliefs. They were held at Colchester and questioned several times by the dreaded Bishop of London, Edward Bonner, who was very active in searching out Nonconformists. Causton and Highbed were condemned and sent to London, where they were held in Newgate prison for fourteen days. They were then taken through the city, bound to carts for fear that attempts would be

Queen Mary, otherwise known as Bloody Mary, whose reign saw the deaths of countless 'Marian martyrs'. (*Author's Collection*)

The plaque in Rochford in memory of John Simson. (*Author*)

The monument in Rayleigh to William Tyms. (*Author*)

made to release them, and delivered to the Sheriff of Essex, William Harris. In March 1555 Causton and three others were burned at the stake at Rayleigh, near where The Spread Eagle public house now stands.

The next recorded local victim of Bonner's venom was John Simson. This husbandman from Great Wigborough was 'examined' at Fulham, and seems to have 'vexed' Bonner with his 'stout and bold' answers. According to renowned local historian Philip Benton, Bonner ended up crying loudly and angrily for Simson to be taken away. The crowd, always in attendance on such occasions, moved away noisily to see the prisoner removed to Newgate and Bishop Bonner seems to have betrayed his cowardice by running for the door to his palace to avoid being caught up in the 'tumult'. Simson's Protestant beliefs resulted in his being burnt at the stake at or near the Market Place in Rochford in June 1555, and a plaque remains there in his name, albeit in a less than prominent position.

Many of the larger landowners took their Catholicism seriously and joined in the persecution of Protestant preachers, which was how William Tyms, deacon and curate of Hockley, and Robert Drake (or Drakes), rector of Thundersley, were singled out for attention. A prominent local landowner, Roger Appleton, was among those who were instrumental in bringing the pair to trial, as was Edmund Tyrell, lord of the manor of Rawreth, whose woods were 'polluted with sermons' by such as Tyms and who put out a dragnet to assist in his arrest.

The monument in Rayleigh to Robert Drakes. (*Author*)

Drake, who also features in Foxe's book, was imprisoned in London for around a year (probably in the Marshalsea prison) and was examined by Richard Read, the Lord Chancellor, in 1556. In spite of a petition sent by Drake's fellow prisoners, he was condemned by Bonner. William Tyms, the curate at Plumberow Mount, Hockley, was deprived of his office by Queen Mary, who was concerned about the large congregations (of up to a hundred) he attracted in Plumberow Wood. He spent some time in prison, and as his physical condition worsened, exacerbated by the cruel treatment he received, so his faith grew stronger. Denied pen and ink for correspondence, he wrote in his own blood to a member of his congregation named Agnes Glascock:

> *Continue in prayer, ask in faith, and obtain your desire. By me, William Tyms, in the King's Bench for the Gospel of Christ.*

Soon afterwards, in April 1556, Tyms and Drake were taken to be burnt at the stake at Smithfield, sharing the same deadly faggots with two others. In 1908 a granite obelisk was erected in Rayleigh High Street in memory of Causton, Drake and Tyms, local examples of the persecuted Protestants known as the Marian Martyrs.

# CHAPTER 3

# An Eighteenth-Century Enigma

The most interesting case in local terms during this period concerned the murder of Samuel Pewter by Robert Wright in 1785. The historian Philip Benton writes of a 'dreadful murder' at East Hall Farm, Paglesham, where Wright was apprehended while thrashing grain in the barn. It seems that Wright followed Samuel Pewter, a butcher's assistant from Canewdon, overtook him and hid in a hollow tree in a field known as 'ware-shot', from where he 'rallied out and accomplished the deed with a hedge-stake'.

The *Chelmsford Chronicle* of 18 March 1785 reported that 'on Saturday last' Wright was convicted of the murder of Samuel Pewter and executed 'pursuant to his sentence and his body delivered to the surgeons for dissection'. It appears that Wright was very penitent, and sincerely sorry for his past conduct and in particular for his inhuman treatment of Pewter, whom he 'cruelly and basely' murdered. He acknowledged the justice of his sentence and requested that no reflection would be thrown on his 'unhappy wife' as she was a 'prudent and virtuous woman'. He refers to his marriage having taken place just a few days previously, but the Paglesham parish records are not able to confirm this. He further declared in court at Chelmsford that his new wife was a 'stranger to the cause of his committing the barbarous deed', but so too are the readers as, frustratingly, no motive is recorded. In fact, Wright declared that he lived 'in habits of friendship' with the deceased and 'esteemed' him as a sincere friend and companion.

The sentence of 'dissection' was intended to reach beyond the grave, allowing no burial site for the guilty party. While the death penalty here is rather more understandable than it was for many other offences at the time, in that it was a brutal, premeditated murder, here we have a murderer with a difference: a man who, to all intents and purposes, was still on his honeymoon. Sadly, a lot of information went unreported in this case.

Wright was the first convict to be executed in the new county gaol at Chelmsford, on 12 March 1785, and he was also the first to die according to the new, speedier practice, a method regarded as 'highly decent, and much to be commended' according to the *Chronicle*. This was what Benton calls the 'drop' and it made use of a trapdoor rather than leaving a body hanging on the gallows. This new facility was located in a yard between the old buildings and the River Chelmer.

Subsequently the event was regarded as important enough for Wright's skull to be retained and preserved in the Essex Museum. The founder of the museum, Thomas Clarkson Neale, was the first governor of Chelmsford gaol when it moved to its present site at Springfield, and the first museum was housed in the parlour of the old gaol at Moulsham (both Chelmsford locations). Although the catalogue entry can still be seen, the skull itself has mysteriously disappeared.

Murderers at this period were only allowed 48 hours between receiving sentence and their death at Springfield. (By the 1880s, this had increased to three weeks between sentencing

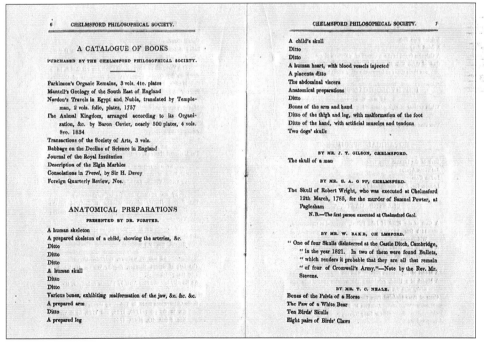

The catalogue entry for Robert Wright at Chelmsford Museum.

(*Chelmsford Museum*)

and execution.) They were usually tried on a Saturday and given the Sunday for repentance. Transportation had been introduced by this time, either to America or Australia, but after the American War of Independence (1776) Australia became the principal destination. This was a rather more humane alternative to the death penalty, and Benton refers to some 'worthies' from nearby Barling being transported but gives no information as to their offences.

Eighteenth-century campaigning, not to mention John Howard's life work on prison reform, had a dramatic effect on national – and local – treatment of offenders at a time when even being in debt was an offence that could land you in prison.

## ANOTHER VIOLENT CRIME?

There is a legend, which may well be based on truth, that another murder utilising an agricultural implement as a weapon was committed on Fanton Hall Farm in North Benfleet in the eighteenth century. The oral history tells of a ploughman who killed his ploughboy with his plough 'spud'. An alternative version relates that a woodsman cut off his young assistant's head because he was not working hard enough, and then hid the boy's torso in a hollow tree, telling any interested parties that the boy had simply run away. The second 'story' goes on to explain the woodsman's habitual drunkenness at The Hart at Thundersley as being the result of hearing the boy's screams in his head. Even now, the ghost of the boy, supposedly headless, is alleged to haunt the Kingsley Lane area where the woods used to be, an area still known by some as 'Shrieking Boy's Wood'. Dates for this event vary enormously, and without names – of either victim or perpetrator – it has been impossible to confirm. But just as there's no smoke without fire, can there be a ghost without a foul deed?

CHAPTER 4

# Highwaymen

In the Hanoverian period (1714–1837) passengers travelling on stage-coaches were at risk from highwaymen operating in rural areas such as south-east Essex. These footpads, as they were known, were also adept at picking off single travellers, and for this they preferred quiet roads and country lanes with plenty of cover to hide in. Such locations abounded in the Southend area. There were also plenty of unmarked roads and hills to render travellers even more vulnerable by slowing their horses down. Those with money flaunted it, but they lived in fear that those without

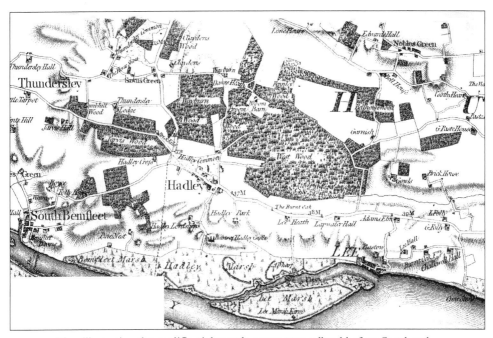

Map illustrating the prolific eighteenth-century woodland before Southend was built. (*Author's Collection*)

money would steal it, and there were plenty of people who had no other way of surviving.

Travellers in coaches between Prittlewell and London undertook the journey knowing that they might lose their money, possessions, limbs or even life. At a time when banks were just emerging, travellers carried their jewellery and cash with them, making them very tempting targets. The limited number of patrolmen and keepers in the thick woodland could not entrap or even locate every ruffian. Waggoners using the roads regularly were often coerced into paying an early form of protection money, any resistance being met with violence.

The well-documented history of Essex villain Dick Turpin is similar to that of most other highwaymen – starting off as a smuggler perhaps, moving on to housebreaking, church robbing and thence to highway robbery. Turpin himself became the ring-leader of the Essex Gang some time after 1735, and then joined the Gregory Gang, which operated in the Leigh and Hadleigh areas, the latter being particularly densely wooded, with Jarvis Wood, Claydon Wood, Broom Wood, West Wood, Pennley Wood, Combhill Wood, Wayburn Wood and Bellhouse Wood all featured in contemporary maps.

It is a less well known highwayman that has the strongest local link, however. He is so elusive that even his name has been difficult to pin down: during the day he was Gilbert, or perhaps Gabriel, Craddock, a man who evidently held down a respectable job as a city financier in London, but by night he was Jerry 'Cutter' Lynch. Although he originated from London, Gilbert bought Leigh Park House and its 125 acres in Leigh-on-Sea (also known as Tile Barn Farm and Leigh House Farm) in 1750. The property was adjacent to the lonely moors of Leigh Heath and the impenetrable West Wood, a convenient hiding-place.

The house was nicknamed Lapwater Hall by the none-too-speedy builders employed to renovate the property. When they wanted more than the three pots of ale a day they were allocated, even though they had not achieved Craddock's deadlines, he told them in no uncertain terms that they should lap water from the horse pond if their thirst was that bad. By all accounts, Craddock was not overly happy with his home's new name, but it stuck and the hall is clearly marked as such on eighteenth-century maps.

Lynch allegedly rode a horse (Brown Meg) with no ears, fitting a pair of wax ones to disguise the animal and thereby avoid detection. Of the two, it was apparently 'the mare who was

Lapwater Hall, owned by Gilbert Craddock. (*Essex Record Office*)

the more handsome', for the rider was massive, 'ugly as a bulldog' and with a coarse face and a squint. While Lapwater Hall was being renovated, no doubt financed by the proceeds of his criminal activities, Craddock/Lynch stayed at The Smack Inn overlooking the estuary at Leigh, and stabled Brown Meg there.

Craddock's friends regarded him as a gentleman of education and breeding, and a skilled chess player. The fishermen in The Smack, however, experienced a very different Craddock, who lashed out with his riding whip when in a temper. He certainly was not the kind of man you would want to bump into after dark.

One night in 1750, not long after buying his Leigh property, Craddock was on the run from the constables once more when one of them managed to wound him with a more accurate shot than usual. In fact, legend has it that this confrontation was with the newly formed Bow Street Runners, which perhaps explains their efficiency. He managed to make his way to Lapwater Hall, but was still being pursued. His only way out was by the back entrance, which he took advantage of, although wounded and bleeding. The constables – or Runners – appear to have given up the chase at this point, but had they persisted they would have found Craddock in his horse-pond. It seems that he had fallen in and, seriously weakened by his injury, had not been able to climb out again. His body was found in the pond the

Illustration of a highwayman from *The Graphic*, Christmas Number 1900, by T. Walter West. (*Author's Collection*)

next day. There will always be a mystery attached to his death, given the circumstances. Would the constables have rescued him, given the opportunity? There has even been a suggestion that he committed suicide by drowning himself once he knew the game was up. Such a cowardly end (or perhaps a romantic one!) cannot be ruled out.

Ironically, it seems that Craddock had been about to marry

Lady Eleanor of Eden House (also in Leigh-on-Sea), which would have enabled him to give up his illegal occupation. Instead, she inherited Lapwater Hall and often stayed there, evidently not bothered by the activities of Craddock's ghost. The highwayman whose luck ran out is buried in Leigh Church.

The suicide theory has also been applied to one of the last footpads in Essex, one Dandy Jack. He is alleged to have hanged himself in 1804 after hiding his loot behind the fireplace that was being installed in the tap room at The Bull Inn in Hockley. Did Dandy Jack know that he was soon to be caught and wanted to make sure no one else had access to the riches he had so laboriously acquired?

As late as 1815, sixty-five years after Craddock's death, the woods in the area were still unsafe. After a property sale at The Lion Inn in Rayleigh, it is recorded that the money received by the vendors was stowed away in their boots for safety before they set out on the risky journey home. No doubt they also armed themselves with cudgels or swords, but this is unrecorded.

Until the police force was established by Robert Peel in 1829 (in London initially but extending to every town within thirty years), it was virtually impossible to catch highwaymen who were not only armed but were especially proficient horsemen. They were of course the original muggers rather than the romantic figures of legend, as the story of 'Cutter' Lynch reveals.

Incidentally, much of his stolen booty was never recovered, and there were rumours that it was probably buried somewhere on the London Road to avoid detection. We shall probably never know. Nevertheless, digging in the vicinity of Lapwater Hall in 1930 revealed a concealed tiled chamber, which could easily have been a secret store for contraband. Sadly, it was empty . . .

# CHAPTER 5

# Witches

Given the level of superstition endemic to the population (locally and nationally), witchcraft was a common accusation from the Middle Ages onwards. John Gaule wrote in 1646 that every old woman with a 'scolding' tongue or a 'squeaking voyce', or who had wrinkles, crooked teeth, facial hair or a squint, in any combination, could be denounced as a witch. Suspicion alone was grounds for accusation and acceptable proof was an 'unnatural' mark on the body, supposedly caused by the devil – hence all those rumours regarding Anne Boleyn, a one-time Rochford Hall resident, who not only had a sixth finger on her left hand, but also (allegedly) an extra nipple to suckle her 'familiar'.

There were cases all over the Rochford Hundred in the many villages that were established long before Southend itself appeared on the county's maps. Between 1560 and 1675 a large proportion of examinations by Justices of the Peace were for witchcraft, although more than half did not lead to a formal trial. In the Essex area seventy-four witches were executed between 1560 and 1645, most of them in the final years as a result of the activities of the Witch-finder General, Matthew Hopkins. Penalties for witchcraft varied through time and according to the level of 'proof', but included excommunication, burning, drowning and hanging. Death by witchcraft was a more common charge than murder in Elizabethan society. The last local trial for witchcraft took place in South Fambridge in 1750, at a time when the water ordeal could establish guilt or innocence, but the craft of course continued for hundreds of years. In this chapter the focus is on the unpleasant face of witchcraft, taking in the nastier specimens of witch and the foulest deeds attributed to them.

The many witchcraft cases recorded in the assize records include a couple from Little Wakering who were tried for murder by witchcraft on 2 March 1573 before Robert Monson

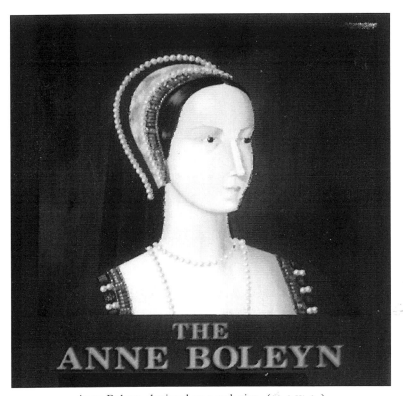

Anne Boleyn, depicted on a pub sign. (*Mark Kimber*)

and John Southcote, judges. A number of such deaths were attributed to William and Margery Skelton of Barling. On 16 November 1568 they were said to have bewitched John Churcherman of Barling, a sailor, so that he 'instantly died'. Subsequently, on 10 July 1571 at Little Wakering they were accused of bewitching Dorothy, daughter of John Fuller, a yeoman, so that she 'languished' until the end of November, when she died. On 26 September the same year Margery apparently used her skills yet again to bewitch Phyllis Pyckett, daughter of Richard Pyckett of Little Wakering, another yeoman, so that she too languished and died. The final charge was that on 29 July 1572 the couple were said to have bewitched one-year-old Agnes Collen, the daughter of William Collen of Barling, so that she 'languished for a long time'. Records do not reveal their defence, but they were found guilty and sentenced to hang.

More lenience was shown in June 1575 to Rose Pye, a spinster from Canewdon, a village notorious for its witchcraft connections. She was indicted for murder by witchcraft, for bewitching one-year-old Joan Snow, daughter of Richard Snow, a tailor, so that she died. Miss Pye was found not guilty. Also in Canewdon, but a hundred years later, young Kathleen Spurrier was found guilty of witchcraft and burned at the stake near the village church. Her ghost is said to haunt the closest pub, The Anchor.

In the Leigh-on-Sea area was the Doom Pond, where witches were ducked. A rope was tied around their waist and they were pushed in to see if they floated or drowned. It was a no-win situation because the floaters were 'proved' to be witches, and the drowned were 'proved' innocent – but posthumously. The most famous reputed witch from this area was Sarah Moore, the 'Sea Witch', who was born at the end of the eighteenth century. In 1867 she was living off Victoria Wharf. With her hare lip and hooked nose, she had the ideal image for a witch, but in her case these deformities were said to appear on the faces of new-born children whose mothers had upset her. One Leigh resident described how her great-great-grandmother offended Sarah Moore by refusing to pay her to foretell the sex of her unborn child; she subsequently gave birth to twins, one of whom had the dreaded curse of the hare lip. Sarah had devised a seemingly accurate method of foretelling the sex of unborn babies, which seems to have been based on mathematical calculations. She could also predict the future by looking into a bowl of seawater clouded by trickling local sand into it.

According to legend, Sarah was responsible for the great storm in the Thames estuary in 1870, in revenge on a skipper who had laughed at her, but church records reveal that she died in 1867. This negates the story that she died at the hands, indirectly, of the same skipper – he struck the rigging three times in anger, and returned to a dead Sarah Moore with three bloody gashes in her head . . . But who knows, perhaps it is the date of her

Traditional depiction of a witch.

Sarah Moore, depicted on a pub sign. (*Mark Kimber*)

'murder' that is wrong. Her appearance and foul mouth were certainly enough to persuade departing sailors to part with coins to avoid her raising just such a storm and wrecking their fishing. There is no doubt she was a familiar figure, sitting by the side of Bell Wharf in Leigh, watching the bawleys sailing in with their daily catches. Fishermen were certainly afraid of her and her reputed powers, and she would have made the perfect scapegoat for many a poor catch or drowning.

George Pickingill. (*Author's Collection*)

Another foul deed attributed to Sarah was that she put a spell on five new-born babies in her dismay at losing her own sons to cholera in 1849, a disaster which denied her the chance of grandchildren. Although the deaths of all five are recorded in the church archives, such a high mortality rate was not unusual for babies at the time. The Widow Moore was also alleged to be able to kill people with fire. In the Leigh parish register of burials at St Clements Church, there are some entries that could be said to substantiate these accusations. On 10 February 1852 Emily Lungley, aged 4, was buried, and the entry in the register has an added note, 'Coroner's warrant: burnt to death'. Similarly, on 27 February 1857 the burial of Jabez (or Fabez) Cotgrove, aged 5, is noted as a 'consequence of being severely burnt by fire'. Note the dates! This is a fascinating area for conjecture, at least.

Another nasty specimen was Nelly Button of Hockley, who lived in the late nineteenth century and was reputed to have the power to hypnotise those she disliked so that they lost the use of their limbs. She got her come-uppance when someone – probably the village blacksmith – planted a 'hedge' of iron knives and scissors around her house so that she couldn't get out, in accordance with the superstition that witches could not cross iron.

Then there was Widow Comon, who was ducked – or bobbed – at Coggeshall after confessing to making a covenant with the Devil (who seemed particularly active in Essex generally), resulting in her killing and laming human beings. She never recovered from the duckings and died as a result in 1699.

The Canewdon area has achieved quite a level of fame with its witch-history, but many of its witches were of a more benevolent nature than those described above. An old tradition says that there will always be nine witches in Canewdon and whenever one dies and is replaced, a stone falls out of the church wall.

The most famous local witch, however, was George Pickingill, born in Hockley in 1816, the oldest of nine children. He later moved to Canewdon. George claimed to be the direct descendant of Julia, 'the Witch of Brandon', who was burned at the stake in 1071, with each Romany generation in between them having served as wizards or witches. During his long life he is said to have established nine hereditary covens in the south of England, all worshipping Satan and practising ritual nudity and sexual inductions. However, while records of Old George survive, there are no recorded details of any foul deeds associated with him. In his case it is the fear that is remembered, fear of the Evil Eye. Just one look and you were ill, until he touched you with his blackthorn stick. He had no need to pay for food or clothes, and never paid the rent on his cottage near The Anchor; farmers were more than happy to provide him with beer to prevent him putting a spell on their harvesting machinery. No one wanted to upset Old George. What is most striking, however, is that Old George's reputation claims him as the last recorded – and perhaps practising? – Canewdon wizard.

He (or at least someone called George Pickingill) died in 1909, negating any claims to eternal life, but the stories about him continued, even from beyond the grave: lightning struck his cottage the night before his death, the shadow of a cross fell across his face as he passed the churchyard on his last day, a skeletal figure visited him in the hospital with his white mice, the horses pulling his hearse escaped from their shafts. How much of this is true and how much simply myth will continue to be the subject of debate not only among Essex folk but also among world-famous researchers into the occult.

# CHAPTER 6

# Smugglers

Smuggling may not go back quite as far as witchcraft (although there are records of smuggling in Bradwell in 1361), but it is certainly responsible for many foul deeds around the Southend area, owing to its location on the Thames estuary. Smuggling was a risky business, but no more so than fishing, so for many this was not a deterrent, although they also risked transportation or even hanging if they were caught. Contraband entering the estuary was often London-bound, and what did come ashore was usually destined for local consumption. Even though the area was not densely populated, there were plenty of eager buyers.

There were eleven inns at one time in Leigh-on-Sea, which mainly provided for ale-drinking sea-farers. Smuggled brandy

St Peter's Church, Paglesham. (*Author's Collection*)

and spirits, however, held a greater attraction for the gentry, who were willing to pay the price with no questions asked.

An early figure of notoriety from Paglesham was William Blyth (1735–1830). This tiny hamlet outside Rochford was the nineteenth-century smuggling capital of the whole district. During one year over 13,000 gallons of wine and brandy were smuggled into Paglesham alone. Indeed, the Paglesham smugglers were so well known that they seem to have operated a sort of ferry service across the channel.

Blyth, known as 'Hard Apple', was a busy man. Not only an oyster merchant, he was also the village grocer and served as churchwarden (doubtless pages torn from the parish records came in handy for wrapping groceries!). Hiding places for his – and his fellow-smugglers' – contraband included the vestry of St Peter's Church, while the dense growth on the elm trees at Pound Pond had the ability to 'hide' £200-worth of silk at one time. His crew was said to have smuggled so much gin into the area that local villagers used it to clean their windows.

Stories abound about Blyth, no doubt many of them having been embroidered over the years. On one occasion he is said to have given the Customs officers so much rum to drink while they were unloading his smuggled cargo that he was able to recover not only his own cargo but also other seized goods under their (drunken) eyes. On another occasion Blyth was captured and put in irons on a revenue cutter, which then grounded on Goodwin Sands. In exchange for his liberty, Blyth helped to save the vessel. He is also said to have taken on a bull that charged at him and the local cricket team (which team incorporated other smugglers always ready with their pistols and cutlasses for interruptions), hanging on to its tail and attacking it with a 'stout cudgel' until it collapsed and died!

Blyth had a reputation as a man who feared nothing, and on whom drink seemed to have no effect. It seems he calmly ate the wine-glasses at the local inn, The Punch Bowl. His wife, Mary Dowsett, was the daughter of another notorious smuggler, who was known to have worked with Blyth. But Blyth wasn't totally dishonest. The oyster dredger he purchased in 1794, the *Tartar*, probably earned him a good living, as Paglesham oysters became renowned throughout the country. On his death-bed, Blyth sent for the local vicar and asked him to read a chapter from the Bible and repeat the Lord's prayer. After this, he declared himself 'ready for the launch', though some legends have it that his last wish was for a brandy.

The Punch Bowl, Paglesham. (*Author's Collection*)

Another well-known, and violent, smuggler was William Dowsett of Paglesham, a relative by marriage of William Blyth. Dowsett operated a cutter with a daunting crew of eleven. Two of his men were shot and killed by Revenue men in 1778 after a chase along the nearby Crouch estuary. Similarly three men received life-threatening wounds when a lugger commanded by another Dowsett, John, was chased for eleven hours in May 1780, although the rest of the smugglers were able to escape in a small boat by utilising their detailed knowledge of the narrow inlets, sandbanks and tides on the mud flats.

Smuggling was not necessarily an-all male occupation, as the story of Elizabeth Little from Leigh-on-Sea reveals. On the surface Elizabeth was to all intents and purposes a bona fide retailer. In the mid-nineteenth century she ran a shop where the Peter Boat car park in Old Leigh is now, selling materials, perfume, gin – all, it seems, contraband. It is probable that Elizabeth was especially interested in the many fabrics and garments that were otherwise subject to heavy taxation – lace, brocade, silk, tapestries and muslins. A secret underground room with direct access to the waterfront was discovered when the original Peter Boat was burnt down in 1892.

Elizabeth seems to have been an early example of 'girl-power', providing the brains behind a complex smuggling operation involving her brothers. They owned a sailing boat which they used to trade between Europe and London, and Elizabeth played an active part in their activities, being well able to handle the boat. She was reputedly educated and intellectual, throwing dinner parties that were memorable for their French wine, good food and brilliant conversation. She was evidently making enough money to be able to employ a French housekeeper.

One particular legend credits Elizabeth with escaping pursuit by turning into the shallow waters of Barling Creek where the coastguard cutter could not follow. The chase had already resulted in her brother Bob (or Bon) being seriously wounded by the coastguards, but she managed to save him – and the contraband – by moving them overland in a coffin acquired from Mr Benniworth, a nearby undertaker. Her disguise as a black-clad mourner seems to have fooled the customs officers. In the meantime her other brother, Will, took the empty boat back to Leigh. (Another version of events has

The Peter Boat, 2007. (*Author*)

her managing both journeys without the help of a second brother, but this seems less credible.) She seems to have been a feisty and enterprising lady, one of the many smugglers who kept Leigh Custom House busy. In 1768 officers tried to deter smugglers by burning a captured sloop after removing its haul, but this did not seem to have the desired effect.

When the demand for illicit spirits outstripped supply, an enterprising young man from Hullbridge set up his own still in Hockley and took cartloads of home-made brandy to Hullbridge. Aware that the brandy was being brought in, the customs officials diligently kept watch along the shores of the Crouch, not realising that it was the road from Hockley to Hullbridge they should have been watching.

The smuggling trade did not always engender violence but it was taken very seriously indeed by eighteenth- and nineteenth-century governments – in those days smugglers were known as debtors to the crown because they had defrauded the state. However, in addition to the loss of revenue, there was a growing threat to public order which needed to be dealt with. More and more draconian legislation was enforced, and more and more customs officers were appointed, and more and more coastguard stations opened. Some of these were apparently adorned with guns, bayonets and pistols, and not just for decoration. The principal coast officer at Rochford station,

The coastguard station, Shoeburyness. (*Author's Collection*)

George Ventris, was often drunk, and in 1845 there is a record of him responding to a knock on his door by firing a shotgun through it, wounding two of his visitors. In fact, men dismissed from the coastguard and Excise services often became 'expert' smugglers.

Although the death penalty for smuggling was extended in 1746 to include those harbouring smugglers or 'preparing' to smuggle, it was another hundred years before the trade went into decline, after free-trade policies were introduced. In the meantime the bodies of captured smugglers who had killed

Smugglers caught in the act. (*Richard Platt Collection*)

customs officers dangled from gibbets all along the coast. Other smugglers who spoke out of turn were ruthlessly dispatched by their peers – there is a story of a Stambridge man found hanging from a mulberry tree after telling tales to the Revenue men. Similarly, in 1934 a group of men digging a ditch in the Rochford area for a water company found a well-preserved male body – believed to have been a man who disappeared after betraying local smugglers a century earlier.

One smuggling gang operating out of Hadleigh and Leigh included Dick Turpin for a while. They lived in the ruins of the thirteenth-century Hadleigh Castle, but the lights they burned there seem to have been attributed to evil spirits by superstitious locals, who accordingly avoided the area. The ruins were on high ground, which was ideal for sending messages by flashlight out over the estuary. John Harvey, one of the leaders of the Hadleigh gang, was eventually brought for trial, with two witnesses identifying him as the man with a 'brace' of pistols who had been running tea and brandy ashore. He was found guilty and sentenced to seven years' transportation.

Local smugglers have tended to be glamorised over the years, despite their violence and criminality, but on a more mundane level some of the less glamorous hiding-places they used still survive. For example, when The Glen in Southchurch was demolished in the 1960s it revealed a number of special cellars that had been installed by an earlier owner who to all intents and purposes had been a local philanthropist. That's when he wasn't heading up a large gang that not only smuggled but also engaged in wholesale theft from ships in the estuary, especially if they were carrying ivory tusks.

Public houses were particularly popular hiding-places. The Bull at Corringham, for example, had sunken chambers under the yard and caverns under the hearth, while The Barge Inn at Battlesbridge offered a haybarn loft handy for storing casks of rum and brandy. The clergymen of local churches were also not averse to turning a blind eye. St Andrew's Church at Rochford had a cavity under the pulpit that was supposed to be used for hiding the smugglers' shot and powder. Perhaps the clergy appreciated the skill and bravery involved, however unlawful.

# CHAPTER 7

# Wilful Murder, 1847

Wednesday 31 March 1847 seemed like just another day to Stephen Parr from Hawkwell as he walked along the thoroughfare between The Old Iron Pear Tree and Great Doggett's Farm in Rochford early in the afternoon. Until, that is, he reached the mead near Doggett's where he saw, lying motionless upon its banks, a man in a smock and hat. As Parr approached the man, he could see he was bleeding from his nose and mouth, and his right ear was completely covered with clotted blood. He seemed to be unconscious, but he stirred when Parr lifted him up and was able to respond to his questions. He managed to tell Parr that a young man had come up the lane with a hoe in his hand and accompanied him towards The Old Iron Pear Tree, but he couldn't remember what happened next. There was a hoe lying by the man's side, which he seemed to indicate was his own, and he was also able to articulate that he thought he had been robbed of a watch and some money.

Parr carried the man into Mr Merryfield's yard and, in the presence of Merryfield's shepherd and another witness the man's pockets were searched, but they found no watch and no money. At this stage the man gave his name as John Terry from Wickford. Parr then carried Terry to the house of Mr Grabham, a Rochford surgeon, and the men were spotted by Mr Starling, the master of the union workhouse, who assisted them inside so that Terry could have his wounds dressed. Starling then managed to convey Terry by cart to the workhouse, where he was attended by another surgeon, Mr Richard Hodges. Sadly, Terry never recovered from his injuries and died a few weeks later on 20 April.

The inquest took place at the Rochford workhouse a few days later and was reported in the *Chelmsford Chronicle* on 30 April. The coroner, Mr Codd, referred to Mr Terry as a labourer, aged 65, and ordered a post-mortem examination.

The jury was advised that the deceased man had not been able to explain exactly how his injuries had been received, nor had he made any dying declaration.

The police had arrested James Willsmore, aged 17, as a result of evidence received, but he was not to be examined at this stage. Mr Codd pointed out that the prisoner had been found in possession of the watch belonging to the deceased, and that it was therefore desirable for him to be brought to court. In the meantime the jury had the opportunity to view the body and hear evidence from several witnesses, starting with Parr, who confirmed that the body inspected by the jury was the body of the man he had found.

Then 11-year-old Emma Scraggs from Ashingdon was asked what she knew of the events of that fatal Wednesday afternoon. She stated that she had been standing at the door of her house when she saw young Willsmore walk by with an old man, going towards the lane leading to The Old Iron Pear Tree. Willsmore had a hoe in his hand, as did the older man, and the time was just before noon.

Josiah Scraggs, a 13-year-old labourer from Ashingdon, then spoke up. He said he knew young Willsmore and had, while 'plough driving', seen him with the man 'about four rods [22 yards] from the lane'. He was only 'two rods away' from Willsmore, and spoke to him in passing asking him how he was, to which the reply was 'bravely'. Willsmore was dressed in a dark brown smock and a straw hat. On being questioned as to whether he had seen Willsmore with a hoe or just the hoe-stick, he admitted that he had only noticed the stick but had assumed there was a hoe at the end of it.

Reuben Ong of Prittlewell, a harness-maker, then gave his account of what happened the following evening, 1 April, between 6 and 7pm. He had been at the Crooked Billet public house in Leigh when a young man came in, carrying some bread and cheese, and claiming to have been out of work for some time. Mr Ong, a generous soul, had told the landlord to bring the young man a pint of beer for which he paid. He then listened to an account of how the young man had sold his hoe for 8 pence and had just 3 farthings left, though he did have a watch that he offered to sell. Another man offered 10 shillings but then found he could not raise the money, so Ong offered him 5 shillings although he did not really want the watch. The young man accepted this, and it was the same young man he saw the following day in the custody of the police at Leigh, dressed in the same smock and hat. He had given the watch into the custody of the police and was now able to swear that the watch produced was indeed the same watch.

Typical nineteenth-century labourer's outfit. (*Rural Life Museum*)

Now Abraham Hockley, a groom from Rochford, spoke up. He knew young Willsmore, although not his Christian name, as a labourer residing at Canewdon. He had seen him at about two o'clock on the afternoon of 31 March in The Vernon's Head public house at Rochford. He had come into the pub wearing a short brown smock and a covered straw hat, and carrying a hoe. When asked, Mr Hockley said he had not seen any blood on this hoe. Willsmore had played skittles and had paid for some porter with half a crown. Soon after, a boy had come in and told everyone of a man who had been 'almost killed' nearby, but Willsmore had not reacted to this – he had merely produced a watch which he was trying to sell. This was identified again as the same watch given in evidence.

The next person called upon was Peter Wright of Rochford, horse-breaker. He had known John Terry for twenty years, and on the morning of 31 March, at around 10.45am, had seen him near Lower Hockley Hall walking towards Ashingdon, wearing a long brown smock and black hat. He had been alone, and carrying a stick, but Wright did not know of what kind; he had merely wished him a good morning and passed on.

Mr Hodges, the surgeon who had been called to the workhouse on the fateful evening, then proceeded to give evidence as follows:

*I found him with a cold surface and a feeble pulse, the result of a severe recent shock; upon examining the head I found the upper part of the right ear cut out, and a wound above it, with a considerable degree of swelling all round; it was a small wound; the skin was nearly cut through; at the lower part of the same ear there was an incised wound nearly an inch in length, which extended nearly through the substance of the ear; there were also two wounds on the right side of the forehead, through the substance of the skin; there were no symptoms of compression of the brain; he gradually recovered from the first effects of the injury, and appeared to be going on well. On the 17 April febrile symptoms appeared with prostration of strength and confusion of intellect, and he continued in that condition, until . . . he died about half past eight o'clock in the evening of Tuesday 20 April.*

This surgeon had also carried out the post-mortem examination and proceeded with his evidence as follows:

*On opening the head, I found a hole in the lower part of the parietal bone on the right side, about an inch in length, and the same in breadth; two pieces of bone were lying detached upon the surface of the lining membrane of the skull; the fracture extended through the bone of the skull, and through the roof of the orbit, opposite the seat of injury; there was a slight extravasation [leakage] of blood in the arachnoid cavity; there was also considerable extravasation in the orbit beneath the fracture; I opened the body and found all parts quite healthy; I have no doubt whatever that the death of the deceased was caused by the injuries received. The wounds were such as might have been occasioned by a hoe; I am quite satisfied that the wound on the ear could not have been occasioned by a fall.*

Next up was police constable John Patten, who first saw the man who gave his name as James Willsmore in the custody of police constable Miller at Rochford in the union workhouse. Willsmore was taken into the room where the victim, who was then seemingly lucid, lay in bed. PC Patten asked Mr Terry if Willsmore was the man who had beaten and robbed him, but Terry replied rather vaguely 'that is the man who was with me when I was robbed'. The watch given up by Reuben Ong was produced, and this time Terry said positively 'that is my watch, and I will swear to it'. Willsmore said nothing, even when Mr Terry said, more affirmatively, 'you know you're the man'.

Another police constable, James Miller, said that he had apprehended James Willsmore on Friday 2 April at Leigh, and charged him with robbing and beating a man near Rochford. Willsmore denied any knowledge of the crime, so he was taken to Reuben Ong, who identified him as the man who had sold the watch to him. Willsmore was then taken to the Rochford union workhouse to be searched. A canvas purse was found on him, in which was a key. Miller took Willsmore into the room where Terry was lying and asked the latter, in Willsmore's presence, if it was his purse. He said it was and that it had a key in it; when it was produced, Terry confirmed it as the key to his hutch. (Presumably the hutch was a form of chest in this instance, although it may have been a container for small animals.) In all, 2s 6d in silver was found on the prisoner, plus 4d in copper.

The coroner was now able to comment that it was fair to assume that Terry had been telling the truth. However, Mr

Codd felt obliged to investigate every fact as closely as possible independent of the declaration of the deceased. He wanted to see if the watch could be identified by a third party, for instance, and to establish whether Terry had money upon his person on the day he was found. Further, he wanted a search made for the prisoner's hoe, and for the person who had purchased it from him. The inquest was therefore adjourned.

A Victorian policeman. (*Author's Collection*)

In the meantime, the *Chronicle* ascertained that Willsmore, 'an indifferent character', had been lodging at the ferry-house at South Fambridge, and on the morning of the attack on Terry had left there with a hoe in his hand.

Interestingly, when the inquest was reconvened some weeks later, it took place yet again without Willsmore in attendance. The coroner had applied to the committing magistrates for the necessary warrant but had been informed that the magistrates considered that they had no power to issue a warrant to the gaoler to produce Willsmore at the inquest. In strict law, this was probably correct, but Mr Codd had not anticipated this difficulty. He nevertheless felt it was insufficient to stop the inquest proceeding and the jury members were sworn in accordingly.

The examination of witnesses started again with Stephen Parr, who had found the mortally wounded Terry. It appears that Terry had managed to tell Parr that he had had about 4 or 5 shillings with him, including a half-crown piece.

John Lawrence, a publican from South Fambridge, told what he knew about Willsmore, his lodger. It seems he moved in a few weeks before the incident, and occasionally went out to work with his hoe. The distance from The Old Iron Pear Tree to his house he reckoned to be about 3 miles. When Willsmore left the house on 30 March he owed Lawrence 1s 9d and told him that he would pay him what he owed the following week. At that time he possessed only a halfpenny, which was enough for a pipe of tobacco.

The next witness, George Chandler, a labourer from Runwell, had known the deceased for twenty years, and in fact Terry had been lodging with him for several months. On the evening of Tuesday 30 March he had seen Terry wind up the watch that was now produced, and had seen it several times before in Terry's possession. It was identifiable in part because of a small piece 'picked out of the face against the XI and by a piece of metal fitted into the works which ought to be brass'. He also recognised the canvas purse, the key and the hutch that was produced.

Chandler's wife Sarah was also examined. She confirmed that Terry had been lodging at their home for over nine weeks, and that on 31 March he had left the house with a hoe at 8am. He had removed the hoe from the stick before he left and put it in his pocket, so he was carrying the stick. Then he had collected some money from upstairs, but she didn't know how much.

Terry had indicated that he was going to Canewdon to see his brother and that he would seek out work on the way. She described him as wearing a dark green smock and cord breeches with an old beaver hat. She was able to identify the clothes produced as well as his key.

A new witness in the form of William Thorpe the younger from Leigh, a carpenter, told of an encounter he'd had on the evening of Thursday 1 April. He was just finishing work at about six o'clock when a young man dressed in a smock frock, short trousers and light shoes came up to him with a hoe in his hand which he wanted to sell because he had no food or money. Thorpe sent him to the blacksmith, telling Willsmore that if the smith would not buy it, Thorpe himself would give him a sixpence for the hoe, which he did. He had seen the lad pull out a watch to check the time during this transaction. A brief conversation revealed that the lad was 17, had been out of work for a week and had come from Canewdon. He described him as fair and with light hair, and confirmed that he would know him again if he saw him.

The master of the workhouse, Thomas Starling, told how he had spotted Parr and Terry standing at Mr Grabham's door, and described how he had removed the injured man to the workhouse. When police constable Patten brought James Willsmore to the workhouse on 2 April, he had recognised him because he – Willsmore – had himself only left the workhouse recently. Willsmore was taken into the room where Terry lay, and Starling witnessed Terry identifying Willsmore, the watch, the purse and the key.

After Mr Hodges had confirmed that the victim's fatal wound could have been caused by the eye of a hoe, the coroner summed up the case. The jury almost immediately returned a verdict of wilful murder against James Willsmore and the coroner issued his warrant of retainer to the keeper of Springfield gaol (in Chelmsford). Willsmore was in attendance at the subsequent trial, but offered no defence to Mr Rodwell, acting for the prosecution. This was a case where the prisoner had made very little effort to hide his guilt, but whether that was through ignorance or apathy is not known.

In court the witnesses reprised their evidence and Mr Rodwell summed up by telling the jury that if they were of the opinion that the blow was intended to do Terry grievous bodily harm, they must convict Willsmore on that charge, but if the man had been struck with the intention of robbing him and his death had resulted from that blow, it was in the eye of the law wilful murder: 'robbing being unlawful, death caused in effecting it would render the offender liable to punishment for wilful murder'. If any doubt remained, then he would be pleased to acquit the prisoner. The jury, after a brief deliberation, returned a verdict of guilty with a recommendation to mercy on account of his youth. However, the judge, addressing the prisoner at the bar, told him that he 'must die an ignominious death upon the scaffold'. Although he implored Willsmore to spend his remaining time in making his peace with God, it appeared to have no effect on the prisoner. His lordship then, after expressing his pain at passing such a sentence 'upon a mere stripling', sentenced Willsmore to death.

A mere stripling maybe, but one who was capable of a violent assault on an 'old' man. Philip Benton, the local historian, described the event as a 'brutal murder . . . near Hyde Wood by a youth . . . [whose] victim was an old man and whose weapon was a hoe stick. The price of blood was a watch and a shilling.' This may not have been quite accurate, but perhaps he hadn't read the *Chelmsford Chronicle*.

It should of course be borne in mind that when work was in short supply there was nowhere for people like Willsmore to go for help. Although their parish was supposed to support them, in reality many authorities would drive such people out rather than accept that responsibility. If they left their parish, as Willsmore seems to have done, they would only receive poor relief if they went into the workhouse. But conditions there were regarded as harsh, verging on the unbearable, especially for a teenager.

Reporting in the media today gives much greater detail and wider access to crimes, and it is perhaps relevant at this juncture to refer to an article in an 1851 edition of *The Times*. This refers to a 'disgusting number of women' witnessing an execution – a public event – with infants in their arms and 'gay flowers in their bonnets'. The particular assembly in question comprised some 7,000 people, and was a sort of moving fair with hawkers of ballads and 'all kinds of edibles' – perhaps sharing some common ground with the modern annual Southend Carnival.

The number of capital offences rose through the centuries. As late as the mid-nineteenth century you could be hanged for stealing a sheep. In 1820 Thomas Fairhead, a local butcher, and Henry Gilliot, a Prittlewell shepherd, both in their 20s, achieved the distinction of being the last men to be hanged in England for sheep (and cow) stealing. But the tide was beginning to turn and by 1861 the law had reduced the number of capital offences from hundreds to just four: murder, high treason, piracy and certain arson attacks.

In the nineteenth century a number of local associations sprang up that might be regarded as the fore-runners of today's Neighbourhood Watch schemes. One example was set up at Rochford with the aim of suppressing crime and protecting members' property, and it cost 10*s* 6*d* to join; another was formed at The Red Lion in Great Wakering to give legal help to its members and to prosecute villains.

In 1840 the parish constables were replaced by a full-time regular police force in Essex. The first recruits had to be literate, numerate, under 40 years of age, over 5 feet 7 inches tall, and healthy. The first uniform included a black stove-pipe hat, which was replaced by a helmet after about thirty years. Southend's first police station was built in 1873 in Alexandra Street. In the meantime a county gaol had been built in Chelmsford to house major criminals from all over Essex.

CHAPTER 8

# 'Fratricide at Leigh'

This was one of the headlines in the *Southend Standard* on 21 January 1886 and the paper went on to describe the state of intense excitement in Leigh as the news spread that one of James Murrell's sons had stabbed his elder brother, causing such a high level of blood loss that the boy did not recover, despite the efforts of the local Dr Orme.

The event took place in one of Ferguson's Cottages at the foot of Leigh Hill. James Murrell was reported to be a waterman who made his living mainly by loading barges with sand. His wife and two young daughters also lived in the Leigh home, and there were quite a few other Murrells in and around the town. One of the Murrell relatives, an aunt, always brought presents as well as a sixpence for the two boys, and on the day in question she had perhaps chosen less than wisely for her gifts were two large shut-knives of the kind used by sailors. The boys were then left to their own devices while the rest of the family went out. They were immensely pleased with their knives, thrusting, parrying and cutting away for some time. However, they soon began arguing, and the younger boy, Frederick, aged 10, was locked in a cupboard by William, aged 13. When William finally set his brother free, the young boy retaliated by thrusting his new toy deep into William's thigh, causing the fatal injury.

William managed to make his way next door, where Mrs Sarah Green, their neighbour, shocked by the amount of blood spurting from the wound, sent for Dr Orme. She did what she could for the sobbing boy in the meantime. The time was by now just before 5pm. The doctor did manage to stop the bleeding and carried William back to his own home. However, at about 8pm the boy breathed his last. According to the medical terminology of the period, he died mainly as a result of exhaustion caused by loss of blood. It appears that his last words, spoken while he was semi-conscious, were expletives, as he raised his hand to strike . . . his young brother perhaps.

PC Davidson was called to the cottage, and promptly arrested Frederick. He took him – accompanied by his grandfather – to Southend police station, where the boy was charged with unlawful wounding and later with the capital offence of murder.

According to *The Standard*, 'no such affair' had ever happened before in Leigh, according to the memory of its oldest inhabitant, which was the only 'memory' they had to rely on. (Having said that, there was a record of a Murrell cousin who was caught up in a stabbing affray at The Billet five years previously, and another Murrell cousin committed suicide by drowning herself in a water butt, raising possible questions about mental stability within the family. Indeed, May Murrell was listed in the 1881 census for Rochford union workhouse as a 37-year-old 'imbecile' from Canewdon.)

At the Southend Petty Sessions a few days later, young Frederick was tried for wilful murder in the presence of Mr Tabor, with Superintendent Hawtree prosecuting and Mr Gregson defending. Sarah Green gave evidence to begin with, describing herself as the wife of Edward Green, a pensioner from the coastguards at Leigh. She told of William's arrival at her front door, and how he had collapsed in her house. Another local lad had been called upon to remove William's shoes while Sarah Green held his head, and she was then able to lower his trousers and inspect the wound, but had been able to do nothing other than bind a towel around the leg. Dr Orme had arrived in just 7 minutes. She had accompanied the boy back to his own home and stayed with him until he died. In response to questions, she claimed not to have seen Frederick or to have noticed the cut in William's trousers, as she had been 'so overcome'.

Then Dr Orme took over the narrative. He had found the boy on the floor of Mrs Green's kitchen, 'covered in blood'. A tourniquet had straightaway been applied to prevent further blood loss from the puncture wound, and the boy was taken home. Dr Orme visited the wounded boy several times over the next few hours but had been unable to prevent his death due to 'exhaustion from haemorrhage'. He had not been there at the moment of death. In answer to cross-examination, he suggested that the wound was unlikely to have been self-inflicted owing to the direction of the cut.

At this point PC Davidson, who was stationed at Leigh, described how he had gone to the prisoner's house, where Frederick had pleaded with him not to be taken as 'I will never do such a thing any more'. The boy went on to say that he had 'stuck the knife' into William, but he had apparently not been cautioned at this stage and there was some debate as to whether this statement, together with accusations that William had not left him alone and had locked him in a cupboard, was acceptable 'evidence'. Mr Gregson's objection to this point of law was over-ruled. Only after PC Davidson had heard what Dr Orme had to say had he returned to the cottage and taken Frederick into custody. The same police constable found the knife (the same as the one produced in court) open and covered with blood on the kitchen mantelpiece, and took possession of it. He was able to identify the bloodied trousers as those William had been wearing, complete with a knife, similar to the murder weapon, attached with a string loop, in the fashion used by sailors.

The father of the two boys told how he had left the house just before three o'clock, and was at Hadleigh when he heard what had happened. Mr Murrell had run all the way home and got there only an hour or so before William died. He burst into tears at the sight of the bloodied knife and trousers that were produced in court and in his distress was unable to identify either.

Leigh Hill, Leigh-on-Sea, in the late nineteenth century. (*Author's Collection*)

Superintendent Hawtree asked for a remand to look at further evidence, and Mr Gregson applied for bail. The latter was allowed in two sureties of £20 each, provided by a Mr Foster and a Mr Eaton. In the meantime the young prisoner in the dock was calm and seemingly unconcerned, fidgeting constantly with the guernsey he was wearing.

The *Essex Newsman* reported the case as 'melancholy' and reported on the inquest which took place on 23 January before Mr Harrison junior, the coroner, with Mr Alderidge as foreman of the jury. The evidence was repeated, with Dr Orme able to give more detail about the injury, gleaned from the post-mortem examination. He described the wound as 'three-quarters of an inch long and two-and-a-half inches deep, with one of the veins severed'.

The coroner explained to the jury the difference between manslaughter and murder, and said that the question was which of these offences had been committed in this instance. The jury then passed a verdict of manslaughter against Frederick Murrell who was formally committed to the ensuing assize. Further bail was provided by Messrs Eaton and Choppin.

In February the *Essex Chronicle* detailed Frederick's final appearance in court. The prosecution was handled by Forrest Fulton and the defence by Wightman Wood. The same witnesses repeated their evidence. Yet again, Frederick's apparent admission of guilt before being cautioned was discussed: would the boy have been too terrified by the presence of the policeman to tell the truth? The cross-examinations continued, and there was additional evidence that the boys had been on good terms at four o'clock when they had been seen happily carrying wood 'into Mr Thorp's yard'.

James Murrell, rather more composed on this occasion, was able to state that the deceased boy had been liable to 'torment' Frederick, who he said was generally the better behaved of the two. (Records reveal that in fact neither was noted for regular attendance at school.)

Launching into his defence, Mr Wood explained that children under the age of 7 were considered incapable in law of committing crime, while those over 14 years old and 'of sound mind' were considered to know the difference between right and wrong, but for children between the ages of 7 and 14 it was more difficult to make assumptions. It should not be presumed that Frederick had sufficient understanding of the conse-quences of his actions, nor was it to be presumed that he had not. Similarly, it should not be presumed that the prisoner understood that a knife could inflict this sort of injury. In contrast, it should be presumed that a child between 7 and 14 did *not* understand until the contrary was proved. If the jury thought the prisoner had no intention of doing any harm, they could 'conscientiously acquit him of this serious charge'.

Only a minute or so was needed by the jury to make a decision, and they found the boy not guilty. Frederick Murrell left the court in company with his father, but didn't get away without a lecture before leaving:

> *Let this be a lesson to you for the rest of your life, and whenever you find there is anything among your companions which displeases you, remember to curb your temper; and when you find it difficult to do so remember that it was by your one bit of temper that you caused your dear brother to die.*

Young Frederick was lucky to escape prison, bearing in mind that until 1899 children were sent to adult prisons. Some young offenders at this time also went on to serve long sentences in the new reformatory schools opened in 1854 for under-16 year olds. These were really tough places, with frequent beatings to enforce discipline.

It wasn't until the Children's Act of 1908 that the minimum age for execution was set at the age of 16. By then, of course, executions were decreasing rapidly, both for adults and young offenders, as the number of capital crimes was reduced and public attitudes gradually changed.

# CHAPTER 9

# Goings-on at Shoeburyness Garrison

The year 1874 did not end well for Battery Sergeant-Major Frederic(k) Leu(r)son (spellings vary) of the Royal Artillery, or for Gunner Edward Ives, a private in the same battery. Ives was described by the *Southend Standard* as a 'dastardly fellow', who had rushed at the sergeant-major as he entered the barracks on 21 December, and aimed at him a 'fierce blow' with a sword that he had concealed beneath his coat, inflicting a severe wound in his victim's side. Leuson and his companion, Bombardier Edward Martin, had grappled with Ives in a 'desperate struggle' which had ended with Ives being overpowered, disarmed and secured.

Ives, who had been in the army for sixteen years, was taken under military escort to Southend the next day, and handed over to the civil authorities. Later that day he was brought before Mr Page, the resident magistrate, who remanded him to the Rochford Petty Sessions. In the meantime Dr Hannan, the artillery surgeon, had treated Leuson's wound, which he described as severe but not dangerous.

Even after his arrest Ives had continued to express his determined intention – in no uncertain terms – to murder the sergeant-major, who had, it transpires, reported him for misconduct. Just prior to the attack, Ives had been drinking, so that 'intoxication had doubtless stimulated his desire for revenge'. Quite so.

At the Petty Sessions a few days later, in the presence of Inspector Hawtree, Ives was charged with attempted murder. The magistrates were Messrs Tabor, Page and Baker and Major Tawke, and the prisoner was described by the *Standard* as 'stern, almost morose looking'. There was no prosecutor at this session, and Dr Hannan was not in attendance, having put in a written statement to certify that Leuson was in the military hospital suffering from a severe chest wound, and would not be in a fit state to attend court for at least a week.

The clock-tower (of *c.* 1860) at the entrance to Shoebury Garrison.
(*Author's Collection*)

The Crown Court trial, with Lord Chief Justice Cockburn presiding, took place on 3 March, by which time Leuson was able to give evidence. The prosecution was led by Mr Croome but the prisoner went undefended. This time, the *Southend Standard* described Ives, aged 43, as a 'tall, determined-looking fellow'.

Leuson now gave his versions of events. In November he had reported the prisoner for being dirty on guard, ordering him to carry out an extra guard duty. At about 9pm on 21 December he entered the barrack room with Bombardier Martin, the orderly. Ives had been due to call the roll and was sitting on a form, wearing a great-coat, but 'on seeing me, he muttered something and made a rush at me'. He felt the strike in his chest but managed to seize the blade of the sword that had struck him. He watched as Martin and a few others seized Ives, who appeared to be drunk, and took him to the guard-room. Luckily perhaps, the victim had been wearing two shirts, a jacket and a great-coat, all of which had been handed over to the police. He was able to identify Ives as the man who had struck him.

The orderly, Bombardier Martin, was the next to give evidence. He confirmed that he had gone to the barracks to tell

Ives about the extra guard duty he had been given, before the arrival of the sergeant-major. He saw Ives make a rush at the officer and noticed that he had a sword bayonet in his hand but he couldn't say if he had managed to inflict any wound or not. Martin also confirmed that two of the gunners present, Edwards and Hill, had helped him to overcome Ives and take him to the guard-room. On the way the prisoner had said: 'I shan't do my extra guard now.'

Alfred Edwards confirmed Martin's story, while Henry Hill was only able to add that he had noticed that the sword used by Ives bore the number '49', which was the number of the prisoner's arms.

The *Southend Standard* report of 12 March now refers to a different artillery surgeon, Dr William Campbell, although it is possible that there may have been two doctors on duty that night. Campbell confirmed that he had examined the wound at around 9.15pm. It was three-quarters of an inch in length and half an inch in breadth, and was located two-and-a-half inches below the left breast, just missing the danger zone close to the heart.

When asked by the Lord Chief Justice to give an account of Ives's character, the sergeant-major explained that it was against regimental orders for him to do so. The response to this was a terse: 'If I thought that it would have any real bearing on the case, I should not allow any regimental order or anything else to prevent the information being given.'

Further evidence was contributed by PC William Edward Smith, who had taken Ives into custody on 22 December. He confirmed that the prisoner had spoken to some soldiers standing near the barrack gates, calling 'Goodbye' and adding 'tell the sergeant-major that I wish he may die before I get there' – there presumably being the police station. Ives had then addressed PC Smith directly, stating that 'I wish I had killed him. He may get over it, and I shan't. I wish to God I'd killed him, that's all I'm sorry for.'

Ives offered nothing in his own defence at this point so the judge summed up the case. He left the jury to deliberate while he listened to what Adjutant-Captain Goodeve had to say, at the suggestion of the prisoner. Goodeve said that Ives had only recently had entries against him for drunkenness but he was making some improvement and was due to receive a good conduct stripe. However, he had to admit that Ives had struck a bombardier on the head with a carbine back in 1859, and had been punished accordingly.

The jury then returned the verdict: guilty of assault with intent to cause grievous bodily harm. Ives was then sentenced to ten years' penal servitude. But that was not the end of Ives's story. Only a week later the headlines in the local papers read 'SUICIDE IN SPRINGFIELD GAOL', causing 'considerable excitement in Chelmsford and the neighbourhood'.

In gaol Ives had apparently been of a 'quiet and reserved character' both before and after his conviction. He had been set to work at the pumps from 6.30 to 7.20 on the morning of 9 March, at which time he was locked into his cell, number 54, to have his breakfast. At 8.20 he was summoned from his cell to attend morning prayers, but directly on leaving the cell Ives was observed by the warder to throw down his tin can and 'precipitate himself over the balustrade' on to the asphalt floor 10 feet below. He had apparently dived head first, and although the warder had run to him immediately and turned him over, he was already insensible, speechless and seemingly dying. His collar was loosened, brandy administered and ammonia applied to his nostrils, but nothing was of any assistance to the poor man who merely gurgled a few times before expiring.

The gaol surgeon Mr Carter arrived five minutes or so after Ives had died. He gave evidence that the skull had been 'forced right in from the force of the concussion' and that the 'parietal bone had fractured and the nose had been smashed into a pulp'. The inquest on the body had been held in the visitors' room at the gaol the next day, before Mr Lewis the coroner and a 'respectable' jury.

Captain McGorreny, the governor of Springfield gaol, filled in the background with an account of Ives's assault and arrest. He had arrived on the scene about 8.50, half an hour after Ives had taken his dive, but before he died and before the surgeon had arrived. At this point he described Ives as 'in a dying state, bleeding from the head and mouth'.

The coroner confirmed that there could be no doubt as to the cause of death in this case. Whether he was entitled to a Christian burial was a different issue, however. That depended entirely upon whether at the time he committed suicide he was in a sound state of mind or not. If he were considered of sound mind, and in complete control, known as *felo de se*, then he would be buried without Christian rites. On the other hand, if the members of the jury felt that Ives was not 'complete master of himself' and that his mind was 'in a morbid state', then they were entitled to find a verdict of temporary insanity, which would permit him to enjoy a Christian burial. But the coroner pointed out that to make a decision regarding *felo de se* could not be done accurately without knowing something of the prisoner's antecedents, in other words regarding the possible presence of insanity in the family. So, if the jury felt inclined to return a verdict of *felo de se*, then he suggested adjourning the inquiry in order to give a relative – perhaps his sister – the opportunity of giving some background information about the prisoner. The jury retired to discuss this point.

Fifteen minutes later one of the jurors, Mr Reeve, told the foreman that they did not feel able to give the prisoner the benefit of the doubt without the additional information that a member of his family could supply. Thus the coroner adjourned the case for a few days, and Captain McGorreny telegraphed Ives's sister, Mary Crombie. She duly arrived with two other female relatives, all in mourning dress and sobbing loudly.

Mary lived in Newark, the wife of George Crombie, a bricklayer. She had not seen her brother alive for over twelve years, since he set sail for India with his regiment. As he had served in India for several years, there was some suggestion at this point that the heat might have had an effect on his temperament. The term she used to describe her brother was 'low-spirited', especially when trouble came his way. She compared him with their father, who had attempted to take his life about a dozen times by hanging, having been blind for over ten years before his death in 1871. Further evidence revealed that the father had always been cared for at home, but there was an uncle who 'had to be taken care of'. Another relative said that she knew the family as 'low-spirited' and at times 'excitable'.

The coroner thanked the family, pointing out that insanity was an 'insidious disease' and that no one knew when it might break out, especially if it was already in the family. If the evidence had raised any reasonable doubt in the minds of the jurors, then he recommended that they give Ives the benefit and let him have a Christian burial. Not unexpectedly, therefore, the jury found that the deceased had committed suicide while labouring under 'temporary insanity' and his body was thus able to be interred in the little burial ground for prisoners in Gaol Lane, attended by his relatives. The gaol's chaplain read the burial service.

★★★

For the record, the most unpleasant deaths at Shoebury Garrison were actually the result of an accident on the ranges in

February 1885, during the experimental firing of a new type of shell. A fuse failed and the shell refused to fire, at which point the sergeant-major tried to 'shift' the fuse with a hammer. The result, not surprisingly, was a huge explosion that killed the sergeant-major, two colonels, a captain and three gunners, with several other men being badly injured. The 'medical gentlemen of Southend' who rendered their services to the horrifically

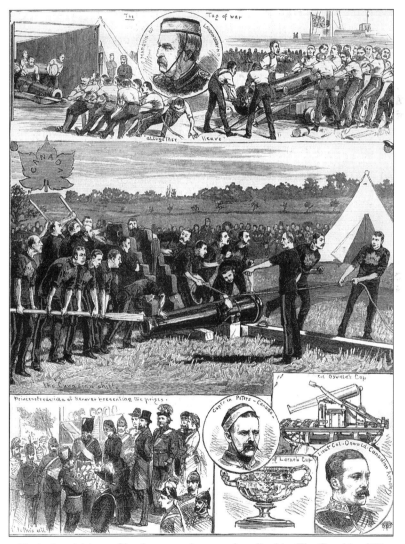

Typical activities at Shoebury garrison, as described in *The Graphic* of 20 August 1881. (*Author's Collection*)

wounded men on the day in question were afterwards granted honorary membership of the Mess. The incident was so serious that Queen Victoria sent her condolences to the garrison and to the widows of the men involved, and the town closed on the day of the funeral in tribute. A plaque was placed in the garrison church, and a hospital for dependents of military families of non-commissioned ranks serving at Shoebury Garrison was built in 1898 in Campfield Road as a memorial: it is now The Captain Mannering (*sic*) pub.

There had been earlier accidental deaths at the garrison. Three sergeants died in an explosion in 1854, and two teenagers from Great Wakering were killed when they picked up a live shell on the beach in 1855. But the 1885 tragedy was the worst, and the best documented.

A death-stricken soldier cuts his throat was the headline in the *Southend Standard* of 21 March 1889. One of the inmates of the Garrison Hospital at Shoeburyness was Gunner John Gamble, who had served as a waiter in the officers' mess for some considerable time, in which position he had 'gained much esteem'. He had been in hospital for two months after being diagnosed with pleurisy, but, although he was responding to treatment, he had then contracted consumption.

Gamble, aged 37, failed to keep up his spirits and developed a suicidal tendency, expressing the wish to poison himself. Surgeon-Major Connolly and Surgeon Poole, the officers in charge, placed him in the charge of an orderly who was specially instructed to move out of reach all cutting instruments and to give particular attention to what the sick man ate. These instructions were carried out to the letter.

But then Gamble asked his wife to make a special visit to him to cut his toe-nails, which were pressing painfully into his swollen flesh, she having acted as his chiropodist during their years of marriage. The orderly moved out of their way, especially as Gamble said he wanted to make clear to his wife how to dispose of his watch and other assets, which he did while his 'vapour' bath was being prepared, and prior to her chiropody. When she reached into her pocket for a pencil and paper, to write down his instructions, she took out the razor she had brought with her for her work, and put it on the bed, subsequently forgetting all about it.

Soon afterwards, around 6pm, Gunner Peter Kirkness returned from running an errand for Gamble after his wife had left, and saw him on a stool in front of the fire. He thought perhaps he was dozing, but on closer inspection he saw he was in the act of cutting his throat. He 'rushed up to him', seized the razor and shouted for the orderly, noting that Gamble was bleeding 'a good deal'. Surgeon-Major Paul Connolly was sent for, but could do nothing to prevent the poor man's death.

The inquest took place at the Shoeburyness Tavern before Coroner Harrison and a jury. Kirkness described the events of the evening of Gamble's death, and Connolly elaborated on the injury. Gamble had severed all the superficial vessels on the left side of the throat and the trachea (windpipe). Although Connolly had managed to stop the bleeding, Gamble had died from exhaustion an hour and a half later; in any case, he would probably not have survived more than another couple of days. Before he expired, Connolly had asked Gamble about the razor, and he managed to explain that his wife had brought it in to treat his nails and corns, although she had been warned not to bring in anything that could be used to self-harm.

Sergeant Hall of the officers' mess pointed out that Mrs Gamble had hurried back to the garrison when she realised she had left the razor there. Her concern had shown in her direction to him, 'For God's sake, go and get it'. Evidently she had postponed her chiropody for a number of hours at her husband's request so he could have his bath, but had forgotten to take away the razor. Although Sergeant Hall went straight to the hospital, he was too late. He affirmed that he knew both Mr and Mrs Gamble, and he felt she had no intention of leaving the razor behind.

The final evidence came from Gunner Frank Vine, who was present when Gamble died. The poor man had not made any statement, and the jury felt able to return a verdict that the deceased cut his throat while in a state of unsound mind. They added a rider: 'In the opinion of the jury, the leaving of the razor at the hospital was entirely accidental on the part of Mrs Gamble'. But was it? Did Gamble ask her to leave it behind during their moments of privacy to discuss his will?

The *Essex Weekly News* went further, placing some emphasis on the 'sensational' rumours that were already circulating, incorporating 'accusations of a baseless character . . . made by unscrupulous persons against the widow'. Superintendent Hawtree had looked into these accusations which he felt to be unfounded. Furthermore, as Gamble had only a few days to live, there appeared to be no motive attributable to his wife. The gossips had had their fun curtailed.

# CHAPTER 10

# Two Unsolved Murders

Picture the scene: the Weir Pond, Rochford, in the spring of 1892. It's a Saturday, and three carefree schoolboys are playing nearby, doing what schoolboys inevitably do in the presence of accessible, if murky, water. One (Freeman) spots what appears to be a sack in the water, and another (Golding) fishes it out. But closer inspection reveals something gruesome in the extreme. The sack contains the partly decomposed body of a male baby with a rope around his neck, and a large stone for company. Startled, the boys threw the stone back in the pond and straightaway went to fetch a police officer. The officer, Inspector Chase, took one look and whisked away the small body and the now-empty bag to Rochford police station.

Weir Pond Road, Rochford, in the late nineteenth century. (*Author's Collection*)

The inquest was held on the following Monday at the Old Ship Hotel before Coroner Mr J. Harrison junior and a jury, with the foreman named as Mr Walker. It was reported in the *Southend Standard* of 5 May. Two of the schoolboys gave evidence. Horace Montague Norden, aged 13, the son of Samuel Norden, a builder, explained that he had been at the pond on the previous Saturday around noon with his friends. When Freeman called out that he had found a sack in the water, Golding had been the one to retrieve it. Norden had cut the string securing the sack, and Freeman had given it a shake – whereupon a baby and a large stone fell out. There had been no delay in calling the police.

Sidney Golding, aged 14, the son of Farley Golding, another builder, confirmed the evidence given by Norden.

Inspector Chase then described how he had found the body and the bag at the side of the pond and removed them both to the police station. Only then did he take the opportunity to examine the small body. There was a piece of twisted rope around the baby's neck and securing the top of his arms. The bag was unmarked, and tied at the bottom. He believed it to be a guano (fertiliser, usually sea-bird droppings) bag. The only things inside it at this point were some brown paper and straw. The stone, apparently thrown back into the pond by one of the boys, had been subsequently retrieved by PC Reeve and was also produced in evidence and identified as such by Inspector Chase. He himself had not seen the stone initially, but explained that the location of the find had been pointed out to him, at a point where the water was about 9 inches deep. He described the pond as a body of water about 20 or 30 yards long overall, and very shallow, 9 inches being the probable maximum depth. It was shallow enough to be crossed regularly by carriages and carts. However, subsequent enquiries had been unable to identify the child or reveal how the body got into the water.

Mr L.L. James, a surgeon from Rochford, gave evidence regarding the post-mortem he had performed the day before, on the Sunday. He described the baby as a 'full-time' male child, fairly well developed, weighing 4½ pounds and measuring 19 inches long. In his opinion, the body had been in the water for at least a week, or more probably ten days, given the level of decomposition. The only external markings in this regard were that the cuticles were peeling off. There was, however, a slight discoloration around the neck, probably caused by the rope (produced), and some discoloration on the left side of the head.

The umbilical cord had been cut, cleanly and close to the body, but not tied, and the right foot was cut in half and hanging by a 'shred', a portion being missing.

To further examine the child, Dr James had opened the chest cavity. He found that the 'lungs filled the thorax', and he removed the lungs, heart and 'glands' to see if they floated in water – which they did. Even a small piece of the lung floated, and it continued to do so even when being squeezed out very tightly in a towel. Decomposition had not set in with respect to the lungs, and 'the heart was full of blood'. Examination of the stomach revealed only that it was 'full of flatulencies', but the skull revealed the most damning evidence of all.

The doctor had removed the scalp in order to examine the tiny skull closely, and had found a fracture on the 'left parietal' bone which had split into two, with the fracture extending to the occipital bone and left temple. The corresponding portion of the scalp had a large clot of blood beneath it and the 'brain was very much congealed on the left side'. He had also removed some of the skin on the neck and found that the blood vessels had been ruptured.

Giving his opinion, he felt that the marks on the scalp were the result of violence inflicted during life because of the large amount of coagulated blood on the scalp. The cause of death was most likely the injury to the skull, or else strangulation. The blow on the head was a very heavy one, probably inflicted almost immediately at birth, with the rope put round the baby's neck to finish the job. It seemed unlikely that the child had lived more than a few minutes.

The coroner now addressed the jury, explaining that they could either return an open verdict, thus leaving the police to make further enquiries, or if they felt there was a chance of further clues being obtained as to how the child got into the water, then he would be pleased to adjourn. While they were considering the options, one of the jury pointed out to Inspector Chase that a stranger had been spotted a week earlier on the adjacent road, a woman, seemingly very tired, accompanied by a man. Inspector Chase had not heard this, but confirmed that he would investigate the sighting. Before deciding on an adjournment, however, another member of the jury asked if they needed to be present. The coroner informed him that they would all need to attend the adjournment, and this seemed to settle the question, an open verdict being decided upon . . .

In his summing up the coroner reminded the jury that the

doctor had said that the child had lived, if only briefly, and had met its death by 'foul means' and thus their verdict would be one of wilful murder against some person or persons unknown. The jury members were happy to confirm the coroner's suggestion, and the headline in the *Standard* read 'Wilful Murder, Infanticide at Rochford'.

The police continued their enquiries, but concluded the mother was not a Rochford resident. One reason for this was the location chosen to dispose of the body – a local person would have known how shallow the pond was, and would have used the River Roach or the tideway in the neighbourhood of Southend instead. They were convinced that the child had been brought to the pond from outside the area. Inspector Chase had managed to trace the strangers who had passed through the town a few days before the discovery of the sack, but they had been cleared of any involvement.

★★★★

In contrast to this poor baby, the mystery of Emma Hunt's death garnered a great deal of news coverage in 1893. It was also one of the first cases where local reportage incorporated artistic drawings of the location – and there was even a map in the *Essex Weekly News* on 2 June. The initial headlines reported the 'shocking discovery' of 'A Woman found in a pond with her head nearly half cut off'. She had been discovered around 5pm on Saturday 20 May, her body lying face down in the water. A labourer, Alfred Hazell, made the discovery, and had been 'horrified' when he approached the body and turned it over to find that her throat was 'cut from ear to ear', with the head 'half-severed' from the trunk.

The villagers of Rochford appear to have been in a 'ferment of excitement' for the next few days before the inquest, trying to decide whether this was wilful murder or a case of a dramatic, and drastic, suicide. As a broken umbrella had been found nearby, and there were injuries to the back of her fingers, not to mention the severity of the deadly wound, murder seemed the most popular bet – though advocates of suicide pointed out that a manic determination to commit suicide would make the brook the ideal choice, in that if the throat-slitting failed, drowning would make death 'doubly sure'!

Deepening the mystery, and the interest in it, was the initial lack of a formal identification of the body. However, Mrs Hunt, a widow and sister-in-law of the local tailor, was found to have been missing from her house in North Street since 20 May. This, together with the distinctive patched boots and the rings she was wearing, seems to have settled that particular mystery.

The young man who had found Mrs Hunt gave a statement to the newspaper. Alfred Hazell lived with his mother in a small cottage in Weir Pond Road near the High Street, Rochford, and had gone out for a walk on the afternoon in question, having no work – he usually worked as a groom – at the time. He had been returning around 4.30pm by way of what was known as the Wilderness, a long path skirting the church. On seeing the woman's body, he had rushed over and pulled her out on to the ground, at which point she gave a couple of groans.

He had then run off as fast as he could to fetch help. In the churchyard he saw Miss Bishop, a lady who kept a shop in the High Street, and shouted to her that there had 'been a murder'. She had called Mr Rowe from the church vestry, and he had told Hazell to get help from town. Hazell had repeated his grisly tale to a couple of signalmen who saw him running, to a railway porter at the station, to the local constable after knocking on his door, and finally to Inspector Chase at the police station.

When he got back to the scene with Inspector Chase, the railway porter was holding the woman's head, but by the time the doctor came – some 10 minutes later – she had died. Hazell said he had noticed the broken umbrella and the bruised fingers, but he had seen no sign of a knife. The body was then taken to the new mortuary at the 'union house' (the workhouse).

Another statement was given to the newspaper by Mr Chettlewood, who lived in the High Street. He had been in the vicinity of the church that afternoon, and had seen a man and woman coming out of the church just prior to the 'affair' but he could not be sure it was the same woman.

Dr James stated that the woman's throat had been cut in a most 'shocking manner'. There were also several other gashes on her right hand and some bad bruising on her hands and face, which was covered in blood. Her false hair had been found floating on the pond. At this stage he could give no opinion as to whether this was a case of murder, and he had not seen any weapon. A nurse at the mortuary made reference to the woman's ghastly appearance. The wet garments were apparently removed and washed at this stage, a very different procedure then than now.

The newspaper went on to report on the search for the knife. Inspector Chase, accompanied by PCs Arnold and Totterdell, had searched for it minutely throughout the following day from 6am using billhooks, shears and rakes. Their search had apparently been watched with interest by a number of interested spectators, but nothing was found.

On the same day, Sunday, the body was identified by Mr Quinton of York Road, Southend-on-Sea. The dead woman was his sister Emma, aged 38. Widowed seven years earlier, she had a 14-year-old son who was employed at the Bon Marche, a drapers in Southend-on-Sea.

There was also a confirmation from the sexton, Mr Rowe, that the couple seen at the time had come into the church as visitors, but he didn't recognise them.

The newspaper brought out a special issue on the afternoon of the inquest at The Old Ship Hotel, to report on the proceedings. The coroner, Mr C. Lewis, had presided, with a jury of thirteen who had inspected the body and the spot where the body was found. Evidence at the inquest was given by postman Thomas Quinton, who confirmed that Mrs Hunt was a dressmaker and 'not subject to attacks of despair'. Then it was the turn of George Benson, a 'one-legged man' who was responsible for the town pump in the Market Square. He had known Mrs Hunt for some years, and said that she had passed by on her way to the footpath, and commented on the 'nice drop of rain we've had'. He had seen Hazell running away soon afterwards.

Hazell confirmed that he had gone out after dinner with his mother and seen two boys cutting nettles near the railway bridge, and joined them. He had seen the 3.30pm train pass and had left not long afterwards, heading towards Rochford Hall and the Wilderness. He then reprised his discovery of the body.

The two boys who had been cutting nettles gave evidence confirming Hazell's story. They were named as Edward William Howard and Henry Haggar, both aged 11. The coroner asked them if Hazell had spoken to them before the inquest, perhaps asking them what they were going to say, but they denied that any approach had been made.

Signalman John Edward Bird confirmed Hazell's version of events. Hazell had used the word 'murder' and had 'seemed frightened'.

But it was the doctor's evidence that caused the biggest sensation at the inquest. Called to the scene, he had found the body still warm but dead. He described the woman's spine as 'notched by the force used', and the wound as large and semi-circular, extending from 1½ inches below the lobe of the left ear to 1 inch below the angle of the jaw on the right side, dividing the larynx above the level of the vocal chords and all the tissues down to the spine. In his opinion, this wound could not have been self-inflicted. This remark caused uproar among those present and resulted in the adjournment.

The search for the weapon began again on Thursday, but proved futile. Superintendent Hawtree, in charge of the case, then decided to arrest Alfred Hazell. The *Essex Weekly News* again gave the most comprehensive local coverage, starting with a statement from the superintendent to the effect that he had been determined to arrest Hazell if no weapon could be found.

Inspector Chase and Superintendent Hawtree had gone to Hazell's home at 9am on Friday morning, at which time he was in bed. As soon as he was dressed, he was taken to Rochford police station and cautioned, to which he replied that he 'did not do it'. At noon he walked to the court between Inspector Chase and Sergeant Spooner, looking rather pale. He was brought before Major Tawke JP and charged with 'feloniously and wilfully and with malice aforethought' murdering Emma Hunt at Rochford. He was remanded to the police station, and was described as leaving the court in a 'perfectly unconcerned manner'. However, it is hard to believe that, at just 16 years of age, such insouciance would continue when he was placed in one of the old-fashioned cells where he was to remain in the charge of a constable for the next five days.

On the following Wednesday quite a crowd of people gathered to await the start of the Rochford Petty Sessions at noon. Space was limited, and special provision had to be made for those concerned in the case, and for the large number of reporters and artists. Once admitted to the Sessions, they could see Hazell sitting with the other prisoners awaiting trial. He was wearing light-coloured trousers with a black coat and black waistcoat. His initial anxiety seemed to diminish as he recognised friendly faces in the crowd, and he nodded and smiled in their direction.

The prosecutor, Mr T. Lamb from Southend, launched into a detailed account of the movements of both Emma Hunt and Alfred Hazell on the afternoon of the alleged murder. It seems that Mrs Hunt was fond of country walking and frequently used the footpath near the parish church for an evening ramble. It was a quiet spot about a quarter of a mile from the nearest dwelling. The total length of the Wilderness path is 970 feet, and it is about 100 feet wide. Halfway along, a secondary footpath leads outwards under a gate, across a field and over the railway into Tinker's Lane, and from there to the Southend Road. Mrs Hunt was spotted during her walk at around 3.35pm by a friend who was on a passing train, and she was spoken to by Mrs Cross, a lady out with her children.

As for Hazell, he was seen going down Church Field at 3.42pm by Mr Hadley the curate, who was on his way to church. Another witness saw Hazell heading towards the Wilderness only two minutes after Mrs Hunt had passed him. Mrs Hunt's whereabouts during the next few minutes were not clear, although Hazell was helping the boys cut nettles with a bean-hook. The boys went to Rochford Hall around 4.30pm to collect their pay, leaving Hazell alone in the Wilderness.

Mrs Hunt was seen again around 4.30pm at the bottom of Church Street by Mr Benson as she passed his garden near the almshouses; they exchanged a few words. Then she passed under the railway bridge heading towards the church walk. Within 15 minutes Benson had seen Hazell running.

Mr Lamb calculated that Hazell was on the spot and had time to commit the murder in the few minutes between the last sighting of Mrs Hunt and his calls for help. If anyone else had been in the vicinity, Mr Lamb felt that Benson would have seen them. As suicide had been ruled out, that left Hazell as the murderer.

The first witness called was Sarah Chapman, a widow living at Potash, near The White Horse, Rochford. She knew Mrs Hunt, and saw her on 20 May between 3 and 3.15pm walking in the direction of the fields leading to the National schools. Questioning by Mr Lamb and by Mr J.E. Searle from London, leading the defence, added the details that Mrs Hunt had been carrying an umbrella and a little woollen shawl, and confirmed the accuracy of the time of the sighting because Mrs Chapman was at the end of dinner, which had commenced at 2.50.

Next up was Henry Arnold, a former engine driver living in Rochford. He had been in the Wilderness that day at 3.15, standing near a gate giving access to the footpath over the railway. He had seen Mrs Hunt coming towards him, but no one else, and had left the area soon afterwards.

Then the Revd Adolphus William Hadley, curate of Rochford, declared that he had been walking from his home

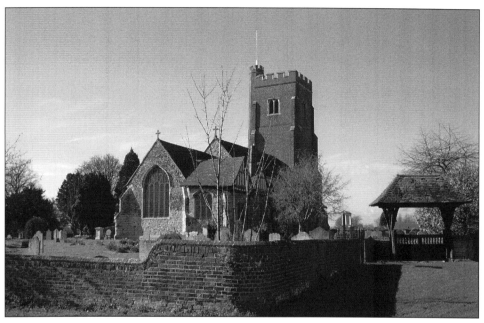

St Andrew's Church, Rochford, has changed little over the years. (*Author*)

near the National schools towards the church, being able to fix the time by the 'half-past-three Up train'. He had seen Hazell going past the stable in the corner of the churchyard a few minutes later, at 3.45 by his watch. Mr Searle asked why he had looked at his watch, and Hadley replied that he had had an engagement for lawn tennis and wanted to be sure he had time to get there.

Miss Eliza Mary Ann Bishop gave her account of hearing screaming coming from the direction of the brook as she placed flowers on her mother's grave. She did not have a view of the stepping-stones across the brook, or of the gate, but she saw a man running and calling for help. The words she heard were: 'There has been a woman murdered in the Wilderness. I have pulled her out of the water,' and then something about needing some help. She was able to recognise Alfred Hazell as he got nearer, and told him to go for a doctor; Mr Rowe then came out of the vestry and also told him to go for help. Hazell ran off towards the signal-box at this point.

The proceedings were adjourned until the following Saturday morning, the prisoner remaining in remand. When in his cell he was accompanied at all times by a constable, and when he was allowed to take exercise in the yard at the police station, Hazell seemed amused by the precautions being taken to prevent his escape: Superintendent Hawtree and Inspector Chase stood in the yard, Sergeant Marden accompanied Hazell as he paced up and down with his hands in his pockets, and PC Arnold manned the gate.

The national newspapers also covered the murder, and some gave credence to a young boy of about 6 who claimed to have witnessed the crime – although only after a lot of leading questions. The boy, called Wakeling, was subsequently interviewed by Superintendent Hawtree, but his story of witnessing the murder was dismissed as fiction. The boy had apparently seen the body of the woman after she had been found, and invented his own version of events.

Similarly the newspapers picked up on a statement made to the police by Mark Chapman, a labourer from Sutton, who had reported seeing a respectably dressed man on the same evening, apparently an 'excursionist', who had asked him and his companion, Mr Potton, for directions. This man had worn a tall beaver hat and was carrying a black bag, but there had been nothing suspicious about him. Certainly the idea that he had 'wet boots and blood-besmeared trousers', as reported, seemed a figment of some journalist's imagination. One reporter had managed to get hold of Mrs Hazell, the prisoner's mother, who – along with her married daughter – had apparently spoken of lunacy in the family.

Hazell had the opportunity to talk to Mr Searle before proceedings recommenced at 2pm, and seemed cheered by his interview, being able to eat some cake for lunch with obvious pleasure. All the witnesses from the inquest were present, plus other well known local residents.

In Mr Lamb's opening speech, he admitted that his evidence was mainly circumstantial, with no witnesses to the actual crime. However, he felt that he had 'strong presumptive evidence' regardless, and certainly enough to convict the prisoner. The only alternative solution that had been touched on was suicide, and this could not be 'entertained'.

The details regarding Mrs Hunt's movements were repeated, as were the sightings of Hazell before the murder. Additional witnesses in this regard included Miss Mary Priscilla Froom, the Board School mistress at Rochford, who was on a train that left Rochford station soon after 3.30; she saw Mrs Hunt, whom she knew, coming from the Wilderness as the train passed the spot a few minutes later. Mrs Cross, wife of Henry Cross the butcher, also gave evidence that she had exchanged a passing greeting with Mrs Hunt that afternoon, on the corner of Tinker's Lane and Southend Road, noting the time as around 3.45, on the basis that it took her a further 15 minutes to get home where the clock showed 4pm.

Mr Hadley's evidence was challenged by Mr Searle, and the curate then admitted that he had only seen Hazell from behind. But he recognised him by 'his attire, his walk and his general appearance', as he had known him for three years, first as a Sunday school boy and then as a member of his Bible class. Mr Searle suggested that if he, Searle, had worn a light suit, he would have been pointed out as the prisoner by Hadley, but was persuaded to withdraw this comment.

Other witnesses repeated the statements they had made previously. Questions were raised in court regarding possible police failings in the case, noting the delay in searching first Hazell and then the brook, the further delay in arresting Hazell, the lack of security at the murder scene. There was no time for further evidence, and the trial was adjourned.

The following day was a Sunday and references to the murder were made at various places of worship. Relatives of Mrs Hunt attended the service at the parish church, where an appropriate sermon was preached by the Revd B. Cotton, the rector, quoting from Genesis: 'The voice of thy brother's blood crieth unto me from the ground'. He made particular links with the timing of such a 'horrifying' event at the same time as 'loving hands' were busy preparing and 'beautifying our altar' for the Whitsun festival. The Revd Cotton also described Mrs Hunt as a regular 'attendant' at the church, who was not, as a dressmaker, in 'embarrassed' circumstances. He mentioned that if she was ever a 'little slack', he would only have to speak to some of the local benevolent ladies and they came up with some work for her. Her great aim in life was to provide for her son. The black suit found at her home was not a mourning suit provided by the boy's mother in preparation for her supposed suicide, but a suit ordered for her son's working day which required respectable, dark clothing.

On this same Sunday the site of the murder was visited by hundreds of people, so rare was this kind of tragedy at the time. Many walked from Southend, with those coming from further afield using the train. In fact, by the evening the railway station was 'crowded with people, who, having viewed the spot, were returning to Southend and Prittlewell'. Even the guard's van had to be utilised to take the surfeit of passengers, reminiscent of today's rush-hour crowds. There seems to have been much discussion not just about the murder and about young Hazell, but also about the location. Although it was known as the Wilderness, the spot was far from dreary and isolated, being a charming area between fertile meadows; many felt that because the area was so open, then if 'no-one had been seen' apart from Hazell, then he must have been responsible.

Before the trial resumed, the *Essex Weekly News* obtained additional information by sending out reporters to make their own enquiries. The Revd Herbert, for instance, made a statement regarding Mrs Hazell to the effect that she was considering 'doing away with herself' because she felt that the people of Rochford looked down on her. Nevertheless, Herbert was of the opinion that a murder had indeed been committed. He had taken the trouble to talk to Hazell before the trial, during which interview the boy had wept bitterly and 'protested his innocence', saying that anyone might have been in the same fix if they had discovered the body.

Even Mrs Hazell was not averse to giving her story to reporters. She revealed that her son had worked as a porter at the Great Eastern Railway at Chigwell in Essex, but had been compelled to leave because of 'convulsive fits'. Although he was a big lad who looked older than he was, he was not as strong as he looked and had been subject to some pain 'in his head' in the days preceding the murder of Mrs Hunt. Although he came home after finding the body with blood on his sleeve, there was none on his hands, and his sister, also present, chimed in with: 'If he did it . . . he would not have gone down to the brook and watched them search for the knife like he did. He would not have had the heart.' It seemed that Hazell's great-uncle was 'queer in the head', his aunt died in an asylum and a cousin had recently been released from an asylum. Hazell's father had little to add, being rather given to wringing his hands and exclaiming 'Oh, my poor boy'.

Although some people felt that her son should plead guilty, Mrs Hazell was adamant that 'My son stands between God and man, and if he is innocent he has nothing to fear . . . even if he gets off, some people will always believe that he did it. His brothers say that after this, if they ever saw anyone being murdered, or if they ever find a dead person, they shall leave someone else to tell the police.'

Repeated searches of the area failed to produce the murder weapon, although several rusty and blunt knives were found once the area had been dredged. No importance was attached to these finds, nor to the old dinner knife that was found buried in the garden at Hazell's home; it had been in the soil for so long that the handle had rotted away.

The Essex Summer Assizes in July that year had thirty-nine prisoners to deal with. As the Black Maria containing the prisoners arrived at Shire Hall in Chelmsford, various men were recognised and greeted, including Hazell, whose mother called out 'God bless you my dear boy'. Several friends shouted out 'Hello, Alf'. As a result, Hazell came out of the van smiling. Mr Justice Matthews started the proceedings by describing the case-load as a 'formidable and discouraging document' which reflected 'the lamentable and discreditable neglect of the moral training of young persons' and left the county 'under a cloud'. He gave his opinion that 'Nothing is more certain than that severity of punishment will not prevent crime' and suggested that 'some of that missionary exertion which is lavished . . . in remote countries' should be provided closer to home. (He made no reference, incidentally, to the increase in crime perhaps being to some extent allied to the increase in population.)

At the end of this busy day, the jury was directed to make 'anxious inquiry' as to whether a 'true bill' (or formal charge) ought to be returned in the Rochford case because of the lack of concrete evidence and the lack of witnesses. The Grand Jury sat after his lordship rose and at 6.30 three of the members proceeded 'to his lodgings' and announced that they had indeed thrown out the bill in which Hazell had been charged.

It still remained for the prisoner, who had been detained in custody that evening, to be brought up the next day to answer the capital charge upon which he had been committed for trial under the coroner's warrant. He was the first prisoner called on Tuesday morning, and, in reply to the clerk of Assizes replied firmly to the charge: 'Not guilty'. The *Southend Standard* described him at this point as 'pale, but . . . quite self-possessed'. The prosecution was conducted by Mr Whiteman Wood and Mr W.B. Daffield, with Mr Horace Brown defending, but the proceedings were brief. Mr Wood referred to the Grand Jury's decision to throw out the bill after a 'very close investigation', suggesting that the petty jury could only come to the same conclusion, and that he would therefore not be presenting any evidence. His Lordship concurred on the basis that only some medical evidence attached any suspicion to the prisoner, where otherwise there was no case to answer. He told Hazell that he would be discharged and declared his hope that the boy would not be treated with suspicion or aversion upon his return home, but rather that he should be offered 'a helping hand'.

At this Hazell expressed his thanks and left the court quietly, attended by his mother and by his solicitor, Mr Searle. Taking Justice Matthews literally, there was a further report a week or so later to the effect that the Revd C.B. Herbert had offered to get Hazell a place at the Carters Boys Home in East London with a view to emigrating to Canada, but Hazell refused the offer.

The case made quite an impact locally, and a diarist named Outten, who took some interest in murder, briefly recording most of the reported cases, saw fit to sum up the case thus: 'After a long trial, he [Hazell] was convicted of wilful murder to the Essex Assizes and then the bill was thrown out and he set free.'

The tombstone of Emma Hunt in St Andrew's Church, Rochford. (*Author*)

# CHAPTER 11

# Two Attempted Murders

## THE GARDENER

A charge of attempted murder was levelled at 68-year-old Joseph Montgomery, a gardener from Shoeburyness, in August 1892. He was engaged to be married to a widow, Mrs Elizabeth Wells, who was referred to in court as 'his intended'. Mrs Wells lived at North Mews, High Street, Southend, and this is where Montgomery went to visit her on a fine August day – but ended up throwing her violently to the ground and attempting to cut her throat with a clasp knife. Luckily for Mrs Wells, several people had heard her screams, and had run to her aid. Three of these men, Garon, Wilson and Osborne, were able to seize hold of Montgomery's hand and wrench the knife from his grasp, although by this time Mrs Wells's neck was badly marked and her fingers were also cut and bleeding from her efforts to push the weapon and the assailant away.

The High Street, Southend on Sea, in the late nineteenth century.
(*Author's Collection*)

At Montgomery's first court appearance in Southend before Mr G. Deeping, evidence of a purely formal character was presented in order to justify the remand, and reference was made to the prisoner's several attempts to commit suicide prior to this incident. He appeared at Rochford a few days later before the bench of justices, with Mr Tabor in the chair. Elizabeth Wells said that she had known the prisoner for about three years. He had called to see her when she was in her back-yard speaking to a neighbour's baby. Approaching through her garden, he had asked after her health, which had not been that good of late, and then manhandled her to the ground just as she was about to pick up the baby. As soon as she was on the ground, he had produced a knife from his pocket, its blade open. With one hand over her mouth, he had attempted to cut her throat saying that he was going to kill her rather than kiss her. Finding the strength to scream, she had been 'saved' by the intervention of neighbours, this being the middle of the afternoon.

The first on the scene were two women who had managed to pull Montgomery off the hapless Elizabeth before the men arrived and restrained him. She gave evidence that her fiancé had actually made three other attempts to kill her, but she had forgiven him, whereas she now realised she ought to have had him arrested. Now she thanked God that she had found enough strength to resist him, because this attempt seems to have been the most violent. Elizabeth admitted that she was afraid for her life should he gain his liberty.

Superintendent Hawtree took this opportunity to ask her if she was engaged to the prisoner, and her answer was: 'Yes, most decidedly.'

The prisoner, in reply to the bench, said he had only been trying to frighten her. He could have cut her throat 'a dozen times' if that was what he wanted to do. He had the time and the opportunity. But on this occasion he had obviously not been expecting her to scream so loudly, seemingly loud enough to frighten 'everyone in the town'.

Next to give evidence was Mrs Annie Sharpe, the victim's next-door neighbour. She was in her garden with her baby, talking to Mrs Wells, when the prisoner came into the garden, spoke to Mrs Wells and put his arms around her neck. The witness thought the couple were about to embrace and turned away to go indoors, but she heard screams of 'Murder!' almost instantly and ran to fetch assistance.

Another neighbour, Mrs Jane Baldock from 14 North Mews, said she had heard the screams of 'Murder!' and ran into her yard where she had seen Mrs Wells on the ground with the prisoner kneeling on her. She went up to them and pulled the prisoner off, although he had a knife and was saying he would kill Mrs Wells. As soon as she had grabbed the prisoner, he dropped the knife and fell backwards. Another neighbour, Mrs Pond, had appeared, but it wasn't clear at this point whether she had also helped to pull Montgomery away. The prisoner interrupted, saying that 'two men who came over the wall' pulled him off, and not the witness, but Jane Baldock stood her ground.

Her evidence was consolidated by Mrs Emily Pond, who lived nearby at 6 Royal Mews. She had been called out by Mrs Sharpe while she was sweeping, and went outside where she saw the prisoner trying to cut Mrs Wells's throat. Mrs Wells was screaming and struggling on the ground, so Mrs Pond hit Montgomery on the shoulder with the hand-broom she was carrying, and then helped Mrs Baldock to pull him away from the complainant. In the meantime Montgomery had been using 'very bad expressions' and had been heard to say to Mrs Wells that he would murder her. Mrs Pond firmly believed that he would have cut Mrs Wells's throat if no one had intervened.

One of the men who had 'come over the wall' gave evidence next. Edwin Ernest Garon of Tyler's Avenue had been visiting Mr Wilson in Market Place and, while they talked outside in the street, they had heard terrific screams coming from North Mews. The two men had run to the wall that separated North Mews from Market Place and saw the prisoner with a large clasp knife open in his right hand, his left hand over a woman's face, obviously attempting to cut her throat. The woman had both hands to her neck. The two men had jumped over the wall at the same time as two women arrived, one with a dustpan and brush who started to whack the prisoner. The women started to pull Montgomery off and the men gave their assistance. Mr Garon had not heard any threats, but he had heard Montgomery accuse Mrs Wells of stabbing him in the side.

The prisoner interrupted at this point with: 'And so she has'. He was then asked by the chairman if he had any questions for the witness. Instead of asking questions, Montgomery accused Mr Garon of giving him 'a good clout on the back of the head, but I don't know what for'!

It transpired that the two men who had gone to Mrs Wells's

aid had then taken the prisoner to the police station. PC Marden, taking the witness stand, confirmed that he had gone straight to see Mrs Wells in the Mews where he had found her sitting on the bed in a very excited state. He had seen the cuts on her neck and finger, which were still bleeding, and had taken possession of the knife that Montgomery had used. PC Marden returned to the police station and charged the prisoner. At this stage Montgomery confirmed the knife as his property, but said he was only trying to frighten Mrs Wells.

Superintendent Hawtree asked PC Marden if Montgomery was sober. 'Yes, calm and quiet' was the reply.

Montgomery was then cautioned, but he had nothing to say. The chairman asked if he had any witnesses to call, but although the street had been full, the prisoner felt that 'they are all on one side. They are all foes, not friends.' The Chairman then told Montgomery that he would be committed for trial at the next Assizes. Montgomery answered: 'I shall get a tidy bit for this job. I am very sorry to hear it. I didn't expect anything of this sort.'

The next Essex Assizes were held at Chelmsford Shire Hall early in December. Here Joseph Montgomery was indicted for 'feloniously attempting to murder' Elizabeth Wells. Mr W. Grubbe acted for the prosecution but no defence was offered. Counsel stated that the couple were widower and widow respectively, and had been engaged until Mrs Wells had broken off the relationship for an unexplained reason. The same witnesses were called, repeating their accounts of the events of the afternoon of Monday 24 August. The only point that was queried by Justice Hawkins was why it had not been possible for the prisoner to cut his victim's throat there and then. Elaborating, Mr Garon gave it as his view that Montgomery had been looking for an opening between her hands to make the fatal cut, but was not given the opportunity by Mrs Wells, who was ably protecting herself.

Joseph Montgomery then launched into a lengthy history of his relationship with Elizabeth Wells, saying that he wanted certain goods back which he had taken to her home when he lodged there four years earlier. He admitted that he had assaulted her and that he had wanted to frighten her, but insisted that he had had no intention of killing her.

Luckily for him, this version of events was in accord with Justice Hawkins' own view. A verdict of not guilty on the charge of attempted murder was therefore returned, but he was found guilty of assaulting Mrs Wells, occasioning her actual bodily harm, and was sentenced to six months' hard labour.

While Mrs Wells had a lucky escape, prisoners such as Montgomery were less fortunate at this time. It wasn't until 1898 that the treadwheel and the crank (which pumped water for the use of prisoners or to cleanse the sewers) ceased to be a regular form of daily labour for prisoners. Each machine had a tell-tale gyrometer, and woe betide the prisoner who did not complete a reasonable number of revolutions. Oakum-picking, another nineteenth-century prison chore, was equally unpleasant, involving unravelling oil-encrusted old ropes. All these tasks took place in total silence, broken only by a session for prayers and for 'meals' – generally bread and beer for breakfast, gruel with oatmeal and onions for lunch, and bread and cheese for dinner.

### . . . AND THE GROOM

According to the *Southend Standard*, the 'usually quiet, peaceful and tiny village' of Sutton, about 3 miles from Southend, was 'thrown into a state of alarm' on Monday 19 September 1892. The reason? An 'Alarming Outrage . . . Attempted Murder and Suicide by an Insane Groom'. The assailant in this case was named as Terence Maguire, aged 32. He had been in the service of the Revd Bredin, rector of Sutton, for about nine years, and the attempted murder was of Bredin's wife Pamela.

It appears that during the previous fortnight Maguire had been exhibiting 'undoubted signs of insanity' and had 'been possessed with many extraordinary ideas'. Mr Bredin, as a result, had written to his sister in Ireland, asking her to accompany Maguire back home, and the journey had been arranged for Wednesday 21 September.

Two days earlier the Bredins had attended some festivities at Southend in connection with the 'reception of the charter' (the birth of Southend borough). Maguire had also walked into Southend. He then bought a train ticket at the London & Tilbury Railway station which would take him as far as Fenchurch Street in London, but he arrived too early for the train and after waiting on the platform for some time seemed to change his mind and walked back to Sutton. He was already back at the rectory when the Bredins arrived in time for their supper. They sat outdoors in the garden afterwards, taking advantage of the mild weather, and issuing an instruction to Maguire to chain up the dog. It seems the dog had other ideas, and this evidently disconcerted Maguire.

Sutton, *c.* 1860, photographed by Miss Gertrude Rogers.
(*Author's Collection*)

Mrs Bredin then went indoors and upstairs to the nursery, followed by Maguire, who bade his fellow-servants good-night. He went down the stairs again to the kitchen, and then returned to the nursery door where he could see Mrs Bredin in the room. It was at this moment that he pointed a loaded revolver at his employer's wife and pulled the trigger. She had an extraordinarily lucky escape, the bullet passing through her hair and just grazing her scalp. The would-be murderer then put the pistol to his own face and fired, the bullet entering his jaw.

Mr Bredin was in the library, but on hearing the two shots and the screams he rushed upstairs and found Maguire lying on his back in the passage, bleeding profusely from his facial injury. The latter moaned out: 'Oh, God, what have I done?' and then began to mutter some kind of prayer.

Mrs Bredin's screams meanwhile had wakened her young daughter, and both she and the nurse were clearly distressed. Messengers were dispatched to fetch Dr Deeping of Southend and Dr James of Rochford, both of whom attended the scene.

Maguire became very violent at their intervention, and it needed four men to hold him down; the decision was made to administer chloroform to enable his wounds to be dressed.

The next day Maguire was taken in custody to Rochford Infirmary, where his wound was pronounced serious but not fatal. Many people called on the Bredins that day to congratulate the rector's wife upon her escape.

Just twenty-four hours elapsed before the next Rochford Petty Sessions, with Mr Tabor presiding. Maguire, heavily bandaged, was brought up and charged with attempting to murder Mrs Bredin. Superintendent Hawtree was unprepared for the case, as he had not expected Maguire to be present. The Revd Bredin, in reply to the clerk, said that the prisoner had been in his employ as a groom for nine years. He had been aware of Maguire on the day in question, recalling that the dog Maguire should have chained up in the stables had reappeared on the lawn where the witness was sitting with his wife and nephew. When they had all returned to the house, Bredin had remained with his nephew in the library for some fifteen minutes, until he heard two shots coming from the floor above. Rushing up the stairs, he found Maguire lying on his back, his face bloodied, and his wife shrieking 'He has shot me'. He then sent for Dr Deeping.

Maguire was remanded for a week in the Rochford Union Infirmary. He then appeared at the Rochford Petty Sessions on a charge of attempting to murder Mrs Bredin, wife of the Rector of Sutton, by shooting her with a revolver, and also with attempting to commit suicide on the same day (a criminal offence until the Suicide Act of 1961). The charges were dealt with separately, the attempted murder being first on the agenda.

Additional evidence came from Mrs Pamela Bredin. She saw the prisoner come round the side of the house, followed by one of the dogs, while she was in the garden with her husband and nephew on the evening of 19 September, probably around 9.30. When she went into the house shortly afterwards, the dog followed her into the kitchen and she gave it a biscuit, in the presence of the prisoner.

Mrs Bredin then went up to the nursery and saw Maguire coming up the stairs. The nursery door was wide open, with a light on, and the nurse was sitting there. She saw the prisoner hesitate at the top of the stairs, then he pointed a revolver at her and fired. There was a loud report, followed by a sharp pain and a sensation of heat at the left side of her head. She exclaimed to the nurse 'Oh, Kate, he has shot me' and the nurse moved to assist her.

A moment later there was a second shot. She saw Maguire fall, and went to his assistance. The prisoner at this point 'began to sob, wiping his eyes with a pocket handkerchief, and seemed much disturbed'.

The nurse confirmed that she was in the nursery when Mrs Bredin came up to say good-night to her baby daughter. While they were speaking, she heard Maguire's footsteps pausing outside the room and called 'Come in', but Maguire hesitated, which she thought was perhaps to allow Mrs Bredin to leave. Instead, there had been a shot, then another. She had seen the flashes and saw the prisoner fall down.

The Revd Bredin added a few details to his earlier evidence. His wife had exclaimed 'He has shot me' as soon as her husband reached the top of the stairs, and he noticed the revolver lying near Maguire. He had sent for the prisoner's sister by telegraph at Dr Deeping's suggestion.

Dr Deeping had arrived at the rectory around 11pm and found Maguire lying on his back on the upstairs landing. The wound, which was still bleeding, was in the angle of the jaw on the right side, with an upward and inward direction, such as would be produced by a bullet similar to the cartridges produced in court. It was consistent with being self-inflicted. Maguire was in a great state of excitement and Dr Deeping had felt obliged to use chloroform to subdue him so that he could examine the wound properly. After that, he had turned his attention to Mrs Bredin, but had found no obvious wound.

Inspector Chase had searched the nursery the day after the shooting but had failed to find a bullet in the room. But when he searched Maguire's bedroom the next day, in the presence of Superintendent Hawtree, he had found a box of cartridges and one cartridge case on a shelf, most of which fitted the revolver in question. Only then was the prisoner – now at the infirmary – charged and cautioned. He made a statement at the time which Inspector Chase read out in court: 'I had no intention of injuring anybody but myself. I did not know what I was doing. I had been in very bad health. I am very sorry I did it, but I did not wilfully do it.' This statement was witnessed, and subsequently signed by Maguire.

Dr Deeping was recalled to give further evidence regarding Maguire's health prior to the incident because he had been attending him for a week or ten days previously for symptoms 'indicating mental derangement'. He had cautioned Mr and Mrs Bredin with regard to him and advised that he should be handed over to the custody of friends. The doctor did not feel that Maguire was able to distinguish between right and wrong at this point.

When the chairman asked Maguire if he had anything to say, he restated that he 'had no reason for it'. He was then committed for trial on the charge of attempted murder, and additional evidence was given on the charge of attempted suicide. Subsequently Maguire was also committed on this charge.

The case followed that of the gardener Montgomery at the Essex Assizes in December, in the presence of Mr Justice Hawkins. Maguire initially pleaded not guilty to both indictments (attempted murder and attempted suicide) but then withdrew his plea of not guilty to attempted suicide. He also pleaded guilty to having committed a common assault upon Mrs Bredin.

Mr Muir, acting for the prosecution, said he would offer no evidence on the charge of attempted murder and a formal verdict of 'not guilty' was therefore returned on that indictment. The judge, addressing the jury, said he did not think they could have satisfactorily come to the conclusion that the prisoner intended to take away Mrs Bredin's life.

The Revd Bredin gave the prisoner an exemplary character, and stated that he felt convinced he was not responsible for his actions at the time of the offence. In the meantime Maguire was apparently 'raving madly' on the stairs leading from the cells, and his shouting could be heard in the court for some minutes before the warders were able to control him. As a result the judge observed that it was evident that the prisoner was in a very bad condition and it was difficult to know exactly what to do with him. 'He must be taken care of, and was there anyone who was ready to see to him?' He felt reluctant to pass any criminal sentence upon him.

It transpired that Maguire's sister had been consulted in Ireland and that she was willing to take care of him in a comfortable home, 'whither she could convey him with the assistance of a friend'. His Lordship intimated that he would leave the case as undetermined for a few days until he had the sister's recognizance in a nominal sum, at which time the prisoner could be released and taken to her home. There, he was quite satisfied, with kind and consistent treatment the prisoner would be more likely to improve than in any lunatic asylum. In the meantime the prisoner should remain in the infirmary at Chelmsford gaol. This course was agreed upon, but afterwards the judge thought it would be better that all the pleas should be withdrawn, and the case left as 'untried'. The prisoner could then be released on recognizances to come up for trial when called upon by his Lordship and a conviction would thus be avoided. Certainly this was the best possible outcome for the troubled Maguire.

# Chapter 12

# The Wife Beater

William Wilkes, a stockman from Canewdon, was incarcerated in Chelmsford prison for over four months in 1898 before his trial started on 1 July. His demeanour had evidently not deteriorated as a result of this experience, and he was compared favourably in the *Southend Standard* with the clear-headed, hawk-eyed representatives of the law in the shape of the judge, Mr Justice Hawkins, the prosecutor, Mr Grubbe, and the defence counsel, Mr Ogle. The Assize Court at Shire Hall was described as 'close, ill-ventilated' and 'full of pigeon holes', but this did not seem to deter the crowds. Wilkes was charged with 'Feloniously, wilfully and of his malice aforethought, killing and murdering Ann Wilkes at Canewdon on the 30 January'. In a loud voice he pleaded not guilty.

Mr Grubbe quietly opened the proceedings, explaining that Wilkes lived at Pudsey Hall, Canewdon, a lonely, 'sequestered' spot with no near neighbours. The household consisted of the prisoner, his wife, two sons, and a lodger named William Cole, who worked with the prisoner. The prosecutor also made reference to the fact that Mrs Wilkes led an unhappy life with her husband. He had been known on previous occasions to have threatened her, struck her and kicked her.

Moving on to the case in hand, Mr Grubbe spoke of an evening a few days before the alleged attack on Mrs Wilkes when Cole and the younger son Ernest witnessed a quarrel between the couple over tobacco. This quarrel ended with Wilkes kicking his wife. Another quarrel broke out a few days later because Wilkes, instead of handing over Cole's 15 shillings wages as usual, handed over only 7 shillings, keeping for himself the remaining 8 shillings which Cole normally paid to Mrs Wilkes for board and lodging. Similarly, he handed his son Ernest 2 shillings and refused to pay his wife the remaining 2 shillings that boy would usually hand over in housekeeping. Feelings ran so high on this occasion in the household that Cole

Canewdon in the early twentieth century. (*Author's Collection*)

slept away from home that night. This argument certainly seemed to be a factor in what followed the next day, Sunday 30 January.

Dinner was amicable enough, taking place between 3 and 4pm. The three younger men then left to attend to their various occupations in connection with the sheep and cattle, with Cole tending to the horses in the yard. Some time later Cole heard screams coming from the area near the gate by the privet hedge. He went to investigate and saw Mrs Wilkes lying on the ground; he watched her get to her feet and then saw Wilkes strike her in the face more than once until she fell down again, her face bloodied around the eyes and nose.

When Cole approached Wilkes to tell him he ought to be ashamed of his behaviour, Wilkes turned on him, prompting Cole to run away as fast as he could towards a low-lying meadow called the Marsh. Wilkes managed to catch him up and knocked him down with a single blow, before disappearing inside a shed adjoining Shuttleworth's, the neighbouring farm.

In the meantime the elder son Frank had been waiting on a stile for Cole, because they had agreed to meet up to work together. Cole spotted him and ran towards him. The pair of them then ran back across the Marsh and hid behind a haystack at Shuttleworth's, from where they saw Frank's mother retrieve a shawl from the family home and walk sharply up the Chase, having presumably taken this opportunity to escape. Hiding again, they heard more screams, prompting Frank to call out to his father, but the screams continued for a short while before silence suddenly descended.

Thinking all was well, the boys moved away to attend to their cattle at Canewdon Hall. Young Ernest, however, had witnessed the whole confrontation between his parents, watching through a hole in the gate when he should have been driving cattle. He saw his father striking his mother until she fell down several times, and seemed no longer able to get to her feet. At this point it seems that Wilkes began kicking her violently. He then picked her up, threw her down again and continued kicking her until the screams stopped. After that, he dragged her into the house and left the building soon afterwards. Ernest took some milk into the house, which was part of his duties, and approached his mother who was on the sofa. However, when he spoke to her, she did not answer. He had to return to his duties, but while driving some sheep along the Chase he picked up the skirt of a woman's dress, minus its pocket, and a shawl that he recognised as the one his mother had been wearing.

A pair of heavy boots was produced in court, and Ernest was able to identify them as the very boots Wilkes had been wearing on that Sunday. Mr Grubbe mentioned that the prisoner had been wearing a light jacket over the top of another at the time of the assault, but when he left the house the top jacket had been removed and left by the sofa on which Mrs Wilkes was lying. Ernest had also replaced the shawl and the skirt he had found near the sofa.

Ernest later met up with his brother and Cole, and they invested in some brandy at the Chequers before returning to Pudsey Hall, telling a policeman on the way about what had happened. The policeman looked through the window and saw Mrs Wilkes, and after investigating further sent to Rochford for a doctor and for assistance. Mr Wilkes had already returned to the room and was sitting there, smoking. Inspector Chase and Dr Lamb arrived in due course. Once Dr Lamb had pronounced Mrs Wilkes dead, her husband was arrested, only commenting that he thought she had had a fit, and he didn't 'see where' he had caused her death.

A surveyor from Southend, Arthur Cayton, now said that he had made a plan of the house, premises and its surroundings. From the doors to the spot where the woman fell was 115 feet, with nothing in between to impede anyone's vision. This was an important point given the evidence of the family members who were spread around the premises at the time of the assault.

At this point William Cole gave evidence about the assault he had seen by the gate, following which he had confronted Wilkes – apparently sober at the time – who had sworn at him and hit him, continuing to holler after him as he made his way to meet Frank Wilkes. He confirmed that Frank had called out to his father, following more screams, asking Wilkes to hit him rather than his mother, but this didn't have the desired effect.

In defence, Mr Ogle asked Cole how long he had known Wilkes and if he had seen him assault his wife before. Cole confirmed that he had known the defendant five years, and had not seen any violence towards his wife until the row over tobacco a few days before this final confrontation. Mr Ogle also referred to some horses that had gone missing that very afternoon on the marshes, and suggested that it could have been the horses that had knocked her down, but Cole insisted that they had been a mile away from the scene.

Additional evidence came from Frank Wilkes, who had spoken to his father after the fatal assault, in the presence of PC Budd, while they were awaiting the doctor and the inspector. Apparently Mr Wilkes had said that he wished that his wife would either move or speak. He also said 'I have never seen her like that before; have you, Frank?' However, Frank, in response to cross-examination, did not feel able to confirm definitely – given the months that had since passed – whether the word 'never' had actually been used, its absence being of some significance. But he was able to state that his mother's face was covered in blood and that he had never known her to have a fit of any kind. He told the court that his father, as a result of an earlier argument, had not been on speaking terms with his mother over that particular weekend. More significantly, when asked by his Lordship whether he had seen his mother in a similar state before, he confessed that he had, but not so badly or for so long, and on other occasions it had been as a result of being knocked about by his father.

Young Ernest, aged 12, was able to confirm that he had seen

the bruise on his mother's thigh following their argument about tobacco on the Thursday before she died. He also confirmed that his wages were usually given to him by his father, having been passed on by Mr Whitwell, but on that weekend he had only received 2 of the usual 4 shillings. The boy was cross-examined closely about the violent scene he had witnessed through the gate, and added that his father, as well as swearing at his mother, had also told her he would kill her.

PC Budd reprised his finding of the body, although he hadn't realised the woman was dead until the doctor arrived. The next morning he had searched the lane and found a pad of hair, some pieces of braid, some hairpins and the catch from a purse. He had found the woman's skirt pocket in the prisoner's light jacket with the purses inside. Mrs Wilkes's skirt and shawl were found near her body, as evidenced by Ernest. The pocket and skirt were inspected in court to reinforce the fact that the one had originally been attached to the other.

The doctor's evidence followed PC Budd's. He felt that Mrs Wilkes had been dead some three hours by the time he arrived, with rigor mortis having set in. There was some blood on her face and an abrasion on the left cheek. At the post-mortem examination the following Thursday he had found further bruises on the face and a cut on the left orbit with bruising all around this eye. On opening the face, he found that the left cheek-bone was broken, lying loose in the cheek, and this piece of evidence caused uproar in the court-room. When all was quiet again he confirmed that violence had definitely been used to break the cheekbone, and that the bridge of the nose was also broken to pieces, which caused another temporary sensation. Great force had been used to cause such injuries to the poor woman. The floor of the skull was also affected, her collar bone was broken and the fifth rib on the right was broken, the latter probably caused by a kick. Her spleen was also ruptured, as the result of a kick or similar blow.

In his opinion death would have followed almost directly after the rupture of the spleen, as a result of shock, although the injuries to the brain were just as serious. Upon being cross-examined, he admitted that it was possible, but unlikely, for the kicks to have been administered after death, although some of the injuries could as easily have been caused by a horse as by a boot. However, the facial injuries were not consistent with a kick from a horse, which would have fractured the whole face. In his opinion the injuries were inflicted by a fist.

The whole sad story gradually came out. Wilkes had harboured a strong resentment against his wife stemming from the quarrel about his tobacco a few days before he attacked her so violently. While it was hardly a strong motive, it seems to have been the best that anyone could muster, although the *Southend Standard* of 14 July suggested that Wilkes was jealous of Cole because Mrs Wilkes looked after the lodger better than she did her husband. Mr Grubbe gave it as his opinion that there was only one possible verdict for the jury to arrive at, and that was one of wilful murder.

In summing up, Mr Ogle explained how rare it was to find a murder where there had been an eye-witness, rather than having to rely on circumstantial evidence. What he did feel the jury ought to consider, however, was a charge of manslaughter rather than murder. He described the defendant as a man who gave way to ungovernable temper, but said he was not a habitually cruel man. Wilkes owned a double-barrelled shotgun, which he used for shooting rabbits and birds, and Mr Ogle felt that he would have used this if he was truly planning to murder his wife. It was also possible that there had been some provocation prior to the final assault, which would also make manslaughter a more appropriate verdict. He did not accept the idea of horses being responsible as a serious option, but he did feel a reduction in the charge was called for.

Mr Justice Hawkins expressed his appreciation that the trial had not been prolonged by unnecessary points of law, thus simplifying the case for the jury. Nevertheless, the law said that the slaying of another person was presumably a case of murder, unless the person charged showed by tangible evidence that there existed something by which they could reduce it to manslaughter. In the present case he could not see even 'a particle of evidence' which would justify them in reducing the charge. Even at the last, when the poor woman had been seemingly unable to support herself, Wilkes had been seen to pick her up and throw her down again into the ditch. 'A more atrocious case of cruelty it would be difficult to conceive', especially with regard to the kicking with such heavy boots that she was subjected to when on the ground. The little boy would not want to exaggerate the case against his father, and his evidence should be taken very seriously.

His lordship felt that there was no evidence of even a single word being used in provocation which would justify so much as the lifting of a finger, and he repudiated any idea of the injuries being committed by anyone else, human or animal. He also went on to remind the jury that the repeated blows and kicks could in no way have been accidental, and that Wilkes, instead of summoning help or attending to his wife's wounds, had instead sat calmly smoking his pipe. Wilkes had also not made any suggestion of provocation, his only contribution being that he thought she had 'had a fit'. The duty the jury now had to perform was a sad one.

Indeed, the jury took only a few minutes to return a verdict of guilty. The judge assumed the black cap and addressed the prisoner: 'William Wilkes, the jury who have in the discharge of their duty been compelled to listen to the most painful and harrowing details of your wicked and cruel conduct towards the poor woman, have found, as they could only find, that you cruelly did her to death by inhuman acts of savagery.'

Wilkes remonstrated at this point, with 'I didn't kick my wife, sir'. In response, his lordship had this to say:

> *You have said so. I cannot say that I can give credence to what you say. The jury have taken your case into their serious consideration, so have I, and so has your learned counsel. You have been found guilty of the crime of wilful murder, and nobody can say that the jury have not had abundance of evidence before them to justify that verdict. By the laws of this country the man who is guilty of the crime of murder forfeits his life. The Judge who tries him has no other duty to perform than to sentence him to die. I have no duty cast upon me other than to carry out the law ... the sentence of the Court upon you is that you be taken from hence to the place from whence you came, and from thence to a lawful place of execution, and that there you be hanged by your neck until you be dead, and that when you are dead your body will be buried within the precincts of the prison within which you shall have been last confined ... may the Lord God Almighty have mercy upon your soul.*

As the prisoner left the dock, his brother, who had been in court, called out 'Good-bye, Bill'. Soon afterwards, Wilkes was removed to Chelmsford gaol in a black van, and upon his arrival at his final place of confinement was divested of his clothes and made to put on the prison garb. The execution was fixed for 8am on Tuesday 19 July. On Sunday morning he attended service at the prison chapel, occupying what was known as the condemned seat.

An interesting editorial piece was printed in the *Southend Standard* following this trial. Although some emotive language was used ('disgusting brutality', 'inhuman acts of savagery'), the feature suggested there was ground for some effort being made to save Wilkes's life and replace the sentence with 'many years of the sharp discipline of penal servitude'. The main thrust of the argument used here was that too much reliance had been placed on young Ernest's evidence that Wilkes had uttered those important words 'I will kill you'. This evidence had not been given at the initial enquiry, but only at the close of Ernest's evidence. Without this remark, it could be taken that there had been no intention to murder. Thus, although this would suggest 'manslaughter of the worst possible type', the punishment should be severe but not death, even for such an 'ugly brute as Wilkes proved himself to be'.

Nevertheless, Wilkes's execution was carried out within the precincts of the prison in Springfield (Chelmsford) as scheduled. The usual application had been made for a reprieve, but was declined. He was visited a few days earlier by his father, brother and nephew, but no other members of his family, his mother having seemingly been ill since his trial. His father had broken down when the time had come for him to leave but Wilkes had stayed cheerful until they had gone, when he broke down in his turn, all the while trying to hide his emotion from the warders.

The *Illustrated Police News*, describing the convicted man as a shepherd, referred to the fact that he had enjoyed an occasional pipe of tobacco during his confinement, had slept well on his last night of life, and had had a hearty breakfast on his last morning. Just before the hour of the execution, a crowd of about two hundred had assembled outside. The executioner, one of the Billington dynasty, walked to the condemned cell accompanied by the High Sheriff, Colonel G.B. Archer Houblon, the Under-Sheriff, Mr Charles B.O. Gapp, the prison governor, Major Darnell, and chief warder, Mr W. Box.

Billington first pinioned Wilkes's arms to his sides, then fastened his wrists together. When asked by the chief warder if he had anything to say, the prisoner replied 'No, sir'. The procession, accompanied by the sheriff's marshall Mr W. Drake in full official dress and the Revd L.J. Hudson the chaplain, along with the gaol surgeon Mr H.W. Newton, then made its way to the execution chamber, Wilkes maintaining a 'firm tread' according to the *Southend Standard*.

As Billington placed him in position, fastening his legs and securing the noose around his neck, Wilkes, now tearful, turned to the warder and asked 'Will it hurt very much?' The mono-syllabic reply of 'No' came at almost the same moment that the executioner stepped back and touched the lever, dropping the condemned man 7 feet 2 inches to his death. The *Illustrated Police News* also made reference to 'a thin gauze cap [placed] over the culprit's head' prior to the lever being activated. There was a jerk of the rope, and the black flag was hoisted to signal to those outside that all was over. Death was absolutely instant-aneous and the body, enclosed in a plain deal coffin, was buried within the prison walls.

# CHAPTER 13

# The 1894 Prittlewell Murder

This particular murder is more fully documented than most in the area, perhaps because of its premeditated nature, and the fact that the victim, a young local woman, was pregnant. The murderer, however, who was unanimously reviled in the press, was not a local man.

James Canham Read, a married man with eight children from Jamaica Street, Stepney, East London, seems to have had several mistresses. The unluckiest, however, was Florence Dennis from Prittlewell. Read was described as a serial philanderer, having already been involved with Florence's sister, and having at least one other mistress at the same time as his relationship with Florence, which had started some two years earlier. Such mistresses were initially unaware of his marital

Prittlewell village prior to its twentieth-century development.
(*Author's Collection*)

status, but Florence did find out late in her pregnancy – at which time Read's youngest child was only just over a year old – and threatened to 'publish' his deception, a threat that led to her undoing.

Florence, who was in her early 20s, had been pressing for some assurance from her lover that he would provide future respectability for both her and her unborn baby. She was becoming more and more desperate as her pregnancy advanced, bearing in mind the moral stance taken in Victorian England against unmarried mothers. So when she found out about his wife, this final humiliation caused Florence to become so depressed that she didn't think logically about the consequences of the action she was planning.

Read, a London docks pay clerk, sent a telegram to Florence to arrange a meeting to discuss her situation. She set out on the Sunday evening to meet him at Prittlewell station, and the two of them were seen walking around the area, which was very rural at that time. However, she did not return to her sister's home in Wesley Road. The sister, Mrs Ayriss, went to the police station on Monday evening to report her missing after sending Read a telegram asking him if Florence was with him in London. In the meantime the body of an unidentified young woman had been found, shot in the head, in the centre of the brook in a field on Barlands Farm. Mrs Ayriss was taken to The Spread Eagle at Prittlewell where the body lay, and duly identified her sister.

On hearing Mrs Ayriss's story regarding Florence's last known movements, a search was instigated for James Read. He had sent a telegram on Monday afternoon in reply to the sister's enquiry to the effect that he had not seen Florence for eighteen months, and he had then left his office early. The police were able to examine his accounts on Tuesday morning and found various papers missing, along with £150 cash. Added to that was the fact that he owned a revolver, and the hunt was on. A warrant was issued for his arrest, which described him in some detail as aged 39, standing 5 feet 7 inches tall, with a brown moustache and side whiskers, projecting upper teeth, dressed in a dark brown hard felt hat, a short black coat and vest, light grey trousers, and presenting a smart and gentlemanly appearance.

The inquest was held at The Spread Eagle, with docks police and local police present. Sergeant Alfred Marden gave evidence that the woman's body had been found, dead and cold, with her head inclined to the left in a pool of blood. There was a bullet hole just above her left ear. A large clot of blood was on the footpath, and the grass was flattened from the footpath to the edge of the brook.

Dr Waters gave his account of the results of the post-mortem examination. He reported that there had been no external marks of violence, only the bullet embedded in the brain. He believed that the shot was fired at close range.

Mr Dowthwaite, an umbrella-maker from Prittlewell, gave evidence that he had seen a couple fitting the descriptions on the footpath where it crossed the fields, at around 10pm.

Despite the intervention of the CID, national coverage of the story in the press, wanted notices all over the country, a watch being set at the ports and plenty of sightings to follow up, it fell to Inspector Baker to finally track down Read where he was staying in Mitcham – with his other mistress – on 7 July. He had tried to disguise his appearance but Inspector Baker knew he had the right man. Read was arrested and searched, and over £80 in cash was found, as well as some keys for his employers' safe at the Royal Albert Docks and even a newspaper cutting about the Florence Dennis inquest. Upon his return to Southend police station, Read was officially charged with the felonious and wilful murder of Florence Dennis at Prittlewell a fortnight earlier.

The trial was long and widely reported, with much local interest in the Jekyll and Hyde character who was a sober, educated, respectable husband on the one hand and an adulterous seducer, thief and cold-blooded murderer on the other. Both the crime scene – a ditch alongside the footpath, with a hedge on one side and high corn on the field side – and the investigation attracted a lot of interest in and around Southend. There was even a song composed by one Teddy O'Neale, part of which goes:

*In a pretty town close to the ocean*
*In Essex well known as Southend on Sea,*
*A murder has thrown the town in commotion,*
*As brutal a murder as ever could be.*
*The victim, we're told, has been a young lady,*
*Who had been deceived by her lover, they say,*
*Shot through the head and thrown in the water,*
*Poor Florence Dennis to death led astray.*

Florence's funeral took place at St John's Church in central

Southend, and this is where she is buried. Mrs Dennis had to be supported by her other children, and eventually fainted as the coffin was lowered into the ground.

The trial began in November before Judge Baron Pollock, and the Shire Hall at Chelmsford was full, with London reporters also present not least because of Read's London connection. He pleaded not guilty to the charge of murder, but guilty to stealing over £150 from the India Docks. His private life and sexual appetites were the source of much interest, and he was found to have used a variety of aliases and addresses to cover his tracks. It also transpired that he was providing for at least one child born out of wedlock – at the Mitcham address where he was found.

The defence called no witnesses, although they did try to discount Mrs Ayriss's evidence as her way of getting back at Read following their own adulterous relationship, but the jury took only fifteen minutes to find Read guilty as charged. The sentence, of course, was death. Unusually, the jury members were discharged from further jury service for at least six years because of the stressful nature of the trial.

As for Read, he continued to attract public interest. A small crowd gathered at the gates of Springfield gaol on 4 December to see the black flag unfurled on the flag-post to confirm his death at 8am, but even more came to see his likeness at Madame Tussaud's in London until his waxwork was melted down in 1949!

A 'Wanted' poster for James Canham Read.

(*Essex Police Museum*)

# WILFUL MURDER

## WANTED

For the Murder of Florence Dennis at Southend-on-Sea, 24th June. 1894

# JAMES CANHAM READ

Cashier, Royal Albert Docks. London.

Age 39,   Height 5ft 7in, Hair Brown, Moustache Slight Brown, Small Side Whiskers, Eyes Brown and prominent, Complexion Fresh. Two Upper Front Teeth project slightly, One overlaps the other.

DRESS, Dark Brown Hard Felt Hat, Short Black Coat and Vest, Light Grey Trousers, Walks Quickly, Is of very smart and Gentlemanly appearance.

Has a Gold Watch engraved inside case " Presented to Mr. James Canham Read by his fellow Clerks, Royal Albert Docks, London."

## WARRANT ISSUED.

Information to be sent to SUPT. HAWTREE, Southend-on-Sea.

FRANCIS & SONS, Printers, &c., 56, High Street, Southend and Rochford.

# CHAPTER 14

# Peculiar People – and Peculiar Finds

From the middle of the nineteenth century until well into the twentieth century the responsibility for a number of deaths in the area was laid firmly at the feet of a religious sect known as the Peculiar People (the term then meant 'chosen'). This sect, a spin-off from Methodism, was started by James Banyard, a reformed poacher from Rochford. As early as 1851 local newspapers were describing its members as 'deluded', the main area of contention being their belief in divine healing which precluded medical intervention.

As a result of this belief, many Banyardites – and especially the children of Banyardite families – died, probably quite unnecessarily. An anonymous letter was sent to the editor of the *Southend Standard* in September 1884, allegedly from 'one of the Peculiar People', regarding the death of one particular child, named therein as 'King's child'. The letter maintained that the child had been supplied with every nourishment that could be suggested, and went on: 'I venture to think that in five cases out of ten [among non-Peculiars], the money [spent on 'nourishment'] would be spent at one of the numerous alehouses instead', in effect accusing non-Peculiars of being less caring. The writer even quoted from the fifth chapter of the Epistle of St James: 'Any sick among you let him call for the elders of the church . . . and the Lord shall raise him up.' He – or perhaps she – felt that:

> *though many of the Peculiar People had been under doctor's treatment they have proved it better to go to the Lord our Creator by attending to his Holy Orders . . . the Peculiars have proved the power of God to heal all diseases through these means . . . the death rate of our children is, we are thankful to say, a very low one.*

Whether this is true or not is not known, but there were three deaths reported in the *Essex Newsman* alone between February and August 1886. The first report, in February, described an inquest at Royston on the body of Martha Theobald, just three months old, the daughter of William James Theobald, a farm bailiff in the employment of Mr Wedd of Foulmire [Foulness?] and Great Wakering. The father was the leader of a small sect of Peculiar People consisting of some three or four families.

Theobald gave evidence that the child had been strong and well from birth but on Saturday 23 January she was taken ill. No doctor was sent for. Two other witnesses, the wives of labourers living next door, admitted that the child was at times in pain, especially when she coughed, and that she gradually became weak and died on Thursday 28 January. The evidence of two medical men showed that the deceased had died from 'inflammation of the lungs' and they believed that with medical aid she might possibly have been saved.

The coroner summed up the case as 'one of the saddest' he had experienced, with a 'hapless child allowed to die in pain'. He explained that the law provided that wilful neglect to provide medical aid should result in a verdict of manslaughter. As a result, the jury found Theobald guilty of this charge, and he was committed to trial at the next Cambridgeshire Assizes, but was allowed bail in the meantime.

Two weeks later the same newspaper reported the death of Henrietta Eliza Harrod, aged nine months, the daughter of George Harrod, a bootmaker of Lower Southend. The child had been suffering from whooping cough for three weeks but no medical man had been called in, and the coroner was again involved.

Another report, in a September edition, concerned the death of Albert Benson, aged eleven months, the son of William Benson from Lambert Street, Porter's-town, Southend. The child had been suffering for some time but as his parents were Peculiar People, no medical people had been called in, although the parents had shown the child 'great care'. Miriam Benson, the infant daughter of Walter Benson, died a few days later at the age of nine weeks, again without medical aid and presumably from the same family. No inquest was deemed necessary in these cases. However, another child from the same family had died eighteen months earlier under similar circumstances.

The usual outcome of such trials was that the father of the family was sentenced to several months in prison with hard labour. Such sentences were not generally well-received by members of the sect. Indeed, there is a letter at the Essex Records Office from one G.W. Foote to Mr Justice Wills, dated January 1899 and apparently reprinted from the *Freethinker*, commenting on his sentencing of George Thomas senior to four months' imprisonment, with the 'added degradation' of hard labour for 'obeying the Bible', a shocking indignity in a Christian country. (Mr Thomas had been bound over for an earlier identical 'offence' but the death of a second child a year later resulted in the sentence which so upset Mr Foote.)

Mr Foote protested that Mr Thomas, as a member of the Peculiar People, was a Christian, and he complained that other ministers of religion had made no protest against his sentence, prompting Foote to raise his own voice 'in reprobation'. Thomas had declined medical assistance for his sick child, resulting in the child's death. But Foote felt that such medical witnesses that had been called upon had acted as prophets, not doctors, using 'empirical conjecture' to suggest that their services would have saved or prolonged the infant's life. Although Thomas had lost several of his twelve children, this was a common occurrence in very large families, otherwise,

A group of Peculiar People in the early twentieth century. (*Essex Record Office*)

according to Mr Foote, 'there would be limited room for the human species'. He argued that 'disease was a divine infliction for sin and only curable by divine agency' and went on that 'to pretend that God must be supplemented by a doctor . . . is a shocking blasphemy'. It was an interesting, if biased, argument, but it seems to have made no difference to the sentence imposed on Thomas or other members of the sect.

In 1888 a list of Peculiar People chapels was published. In our area they were to be found in Daws Heath, Rochford, Foulness, Great Wakering, Southend and Hockley, but there were many others in the rest of Essex, as well as in London and Kent.

## A DIFFERENT MEANING OF 'PECULIAR'

As media coverage in the nineteenth century began to increase, more information was forthcoming about the number of peculiar finds – mainly bodies – that were washed up on the shores of the south Essex coastline. The bleak sands and treacherous waters round Foulness Sands and Shoeburyness in particular often threw up mysteries that were destined to remain unsolved. A few examples follow.

One case where the body could at least be identified was that of Sapper Charles Rose, aged 30, of the Royal Engineers. His body was found on the sands by Mr Robinson, the landlord of The Halfway House, Southchurch, in March 1875. An inquest was held before Mr Codd at the Shoebury Tavern. It appeared from the evidence that the deceased and two other sappers had been to Southend-on-Sea from Shoebury on Sunday evening, and, while returning along the beach in the dark, with strong winds and rain prevailing, had ended up in the sea. It seems they had all had plenty to drink, although no doubt the temperature of the water had a sobering effect. The wind made it impossible for them to help each other with verbal directions, and one confessed that he had even begun swimming towards the Kent coast before realising his mistake. Two of them made it home, but not Sapper Rose, who was overwhelmed by the tide. The jury returned an open verdict.

More gruesomely, 'An Extraordinary Discovery' at Foulness was reported in the *Essex Newsman* of 28 August 1886. An old oak coffin containing human remains was found off the saltings of Foulness Point. Superintendent Hawtree felt that the body had probably been buried by the crew of some passing ship, given that sailors had an aversion to burial at sea if it could be avoided, and that the tide had washed away the saltings to expose the coffin. There was no name on the lid, which was removed, along with the skull, and taken to Newlands Farm, about a mile distant, to be properly buried. The event apparently caused a sensation on Foulness Island, but the coroner took no further action, the remains being long past any attempt to identify them.

On Foulness Sands again, this time in February 1887, another body was discovered in a much decomposed state by Philip Cole, a waterman. It was apparently that of a man aged about 50, 5 feet 6 inches tall, and wearing a blue guernsey sweater with a checked shirt and a pair of blue serge trousers under a pair of moleskin trousers, with grey worsted stockings and laced boots. The body was removed to the 'dead house' at Foulness Church.

It seems that the description coincided in several particulars with that of William Halls, the master of a Rochester barge which was sunk by a steamer off the Mucking Light in November 1886. It had been presumed at the time that he had been knocked overboard and drowned. James Smith, the mate of that barge, proceeded to Foulness on Tuesday but failed to recognise the body – perhaps not surprisingly.

The *Essex Weekly News* reported that the body was buried in Foulness churchyard in accordance with the instructions of the

A landing place at Foulness Sands. (*Peter Owen Collection*)

coroner who had communicated with the police. The issue of *Essex Newsman* that came out the next day added the interesting 'suspicious fact' that Mr Halls' pockets had 'apparently been cut off as if someone had taken his money', leaving questions such as 'Was Halls helped on his way?' and 'At what point was he robbed?' Sadly, these questions will never now be answered.

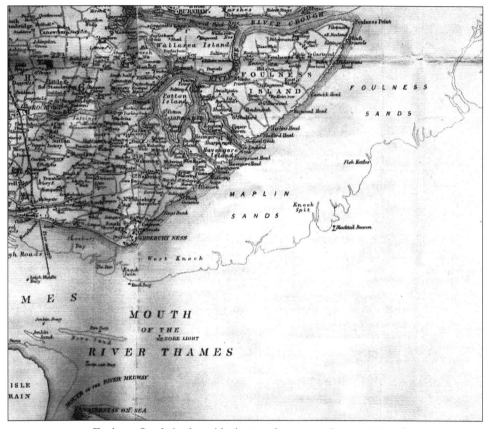

Foulness Sands in the mid-nineteenth century. (*Author's Collection*)

# CHAPTER 15

# Double Tragedy

Mrs Jeannie Tait left her lodgings at 1 Honiton Road, Southend, on the afternoon of Tuesday 25 June 1901 to buy some shrimps, but she never got to eat them. Upon her return, around 5pm, she saw her husband standing on some waste ground adjoining the lodgings north of Marine Park (long gone) with a revolver in his hand. When she saw the gun, Mrs Tait screamed, the revolver was fired three times and she fell dying.

The shooting was witnessed by some passers-by in a brake, who watched in horror as the man then appeared to turn the gun on himself, but no further shots were heard. Instead he turned and fled along the unmade road at the bottom of Honiton Road at a very athletic pace, pursued by the men from the brake and others who had heard the gunshots, all eager to capture the assailant. The area's marshes, hedges and ditches did not slow the murderer down, but he could not shake off his pursuers; instead, he used the revolver on himself when he reached Thorpe Hall at Southchurch (where the golf course is now). The chasing pack, totalling some thirty men in all, found the man's lifeless body in a ditch at the back of the Hall just minutes later.

The *Southend Standard* of 27 June described Mrs Tait as a respectably dressed woman of about 35 years of age, who had been lodging at her last address for some time. The murderer was described as a man of about 5 foot 8 inches tall, wearing a blue suit and peaked cap, who had been seen 'watching' the Honiton Road house on the day of the murder.

A useful eye-witness was Mr Sparham, the brake driver, who willingly told reporters – and anyone else who would listen – about the cold-blooded shooting he had witnessed. He had been one of several men who had jumped immediately from the vehicle, and he had lifted the woman up, oblivious of her blood running down his coat. It was obvious to him that she was dying. According to Mr Sparham, that was 'a good coat ruined'. He, it seems, was the one who had called for the doctor, shouted for some water, and 'was just carrying her off' when Dr Bluck arrived on the scene. Although he had gone to the police station, they wouldn't give him 'another coat'.

Another willing interviewee was Ebenezer Cottee, who had been serving customers in Brewery Road and, on hearing the shot, had turned round to see the flash and the smoke and the woman crumpling to the ground. He had immediately rushed to assist and helped to take her body into the house. He noted that the assailant, after pointing the revolver at himself, had then run off, hotly pursued. John Slade, from Park House, Southchurch Avenue, had also heard the shot and assisted in carrying the woman into the house, at which point she was still – just – alive.

It seems that the *Standard*'s reporter was outside the police station in Southend when Sergeant Lowe and Constable Prime returned carrying the woman's 'gory' blood-stained chemise, bodice and collar. The place where the murderer lay, himself now dead, was described in rather poetic tones in the newspaper. It was apparently then a 'singularly quiet and peaceful' spot, which the builders had 'not yet laid their vandal hands upon'. The report went on: 'The birds were singing in the hedgerow . . . cows were grazing peacefully within a few yards, all unconscious of the grim chapter of human life which had been closed by the death of the man who had rushed past them.' The place where Jeannie Tait had met her death was less delightful – an area of waste ground used for storage by the tramways works, with heaps of gravel and blocks of lava strewn around and heaped up in piles.

Dr W. Cardy Bluck gave his account of events in the same issue. He lived in York Road and was returning on his bicycle from Wakering when he was met by a crowd calling out 'A murder, a murder!' He immediately rode down Southchurch Avenue and found the woman lying unconscious, bleeding heavily from two revolver shot wounds in her head. Although he tried to stop the bleeding, he could see that the woman was beyond any kind of medical help, having been shot in the brain. She survived only another twenty minutes, and then Dr Allot took over and attended to the removal of the corpse to the mortuary.

The story behind the murder was revealed by a friend of the couple involved, Mr Zachelmayer of Milton Road,

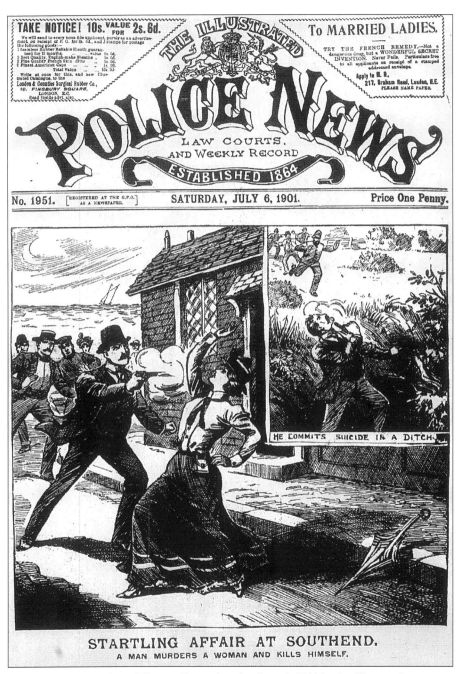

Artist's drawing of George Facer shooting Jeannie Tait, in the *Illustrated Police News*, 6 July 1901. (*British Library*)

Southend. Jeannie Tate originated from Glasgow and had married George Facer – the murderer – some fourteen or fifteen years earlier when he was a sergeant in the Fifteenth Hussars. He served in the Army for twenty-three years and retired on a full pension, later working in London for a firm of cartage contractors. It turned out that it was a bigamous marriage, since Facer's first wife was still alive, but, although Jeannie found out, she continued to live with him for some years. They had two sons, aged 3 and 7.

Mr and Mrs Zachelmayer had known Mr and Mrs Facer when they were living in Leytonstone. The couple had then moved to Ilford, where their family life deteriorated until George Facer was summoned before Stratford magistrates for an assault upon his 'wife'. As a result, he was sent to prison for a month, a separation order was made, and the custody of the two boys was given to Jeannie. During George's imprisonment, Jeannie sold their furniture, placed the boys in a Dr Barnardo's home in Jersey and went to live with her friend Mrs Cummings in Ilford.

Thus when Facer was released, he found he had no home, no wife and no children. Although he managed to trace Jeannie, he could not persuade her to return, and he went to stay with Mr Zachelmayer for a while at Manor Park. In the meantime Jeannie had moved with Mrs Cummings to Honiton Road.

Three weeks before the fatal attack, George Facer had been to Jersey to visit his sons, and while there he had written to Jeannie, apparently begging her to allow him to remove the boys from the home, because he could not do so without her consent. She refused. Coincidentally the Zachelmayers were also now living in Southend, so Facer went to stay with them for a holiday.

The day before the crime, while out for a walk along Marine Parade, they had met up with Jeannie and Mrs Cummings. The encounter obviously upset Facer, who went to bed early that evening, unusually for him. The next morning Facer ate his breakfast with the Zachelmayers and accompanied Mr Zachelmayer to his place of employment, Garon's Toilet Saloon in Southend High Street, returning to their home for his dinner at 1pm as usual. When he left the house at 2.30 he had seemed his normal self, and had talked about returning to Milton Road for tea after going to Hadleigh. That was the last Mr Zachelmayer saw of him.

The initial inquest at the Court House, Southend, was adjourned for a few days to give Dr Bluck a chance to carry out a post-mortem examination on Jeannie Tait. He confirmed that he had found one bullet inside her brain and another bullet wound alongside.

Additional evidence regarding George Facer's death was provided by William Pettitt of Southchurch Avenue. It appears that Mr Pettitt was the first to discover Facer, lying in a ditch and still alive. When Pettitt called out 'Here he is', Facer shot himself behind his ear, and rolled over into the water. The witness then jumped in, picked up the revolver and hauled Facer's body, with assistance, out of the ditch.

PC Carr was the first on the scene after this shooting, having made his way to the area with PC Hutley. He heard the report of the revolver as he approached, and rushed through the thicket and jumped the ditch where the body was lying. Two men were in the ditch, lifting out the body. PC Carr unloaded the revolver, which had six chambers. There were five empty cartridges. He then removed the body to the mortuary in a cart. He found on the body a ticket that gave Facer's name and his wife's, along with her address. PC Prime, who had also been at the crime scene, searched the body at the mortuary and found a quantity of letters, an army discharge paper, a cheque book and two marriage certificates, along with two bullets and some small change.

Mrs Cummings handed over some letters and documents she had found among Jeannie Tate's papers, dated January 1900. One of these, signed by Mr and Mrs Facer, was a mutual agreement that they should separate for a period of six months, with Jeannie keeping the home and children. Another, signed by George Facer, confirmed that Jeannie had been a 'true, loyal and honourable wife', whom he had treated 'cruelly' and whom he had accused 'in a moment of mad uncontrollable temper', and another confirmed that all the furniture at Freeland Villa, Shrewsbury Road, Plaistow, East London, was the property of Jeannie Facer, 'bought and paid for by the fruits of her own exertions independent of my income'. This was also signed by George Facer.

The most interesting documents produced in court, however, were letters written by George Facer on 15 and 16 June 1901. The first declared that 'George Augustus Facer' had come to Southend to shoot both Jeannie and himself because she would not release his boys from Dr Barnardo's

Home for Waifs and Strays, but, having thought better of it, he had decided to 'spare her life' so she 'may get out our dear ones again'. He had decided in that letter to take his own life as near to her as possible, that is to say in her garden, because he was 'broken-hearted'. On the one hand, he blamed drink for his misfortunes, but he also felt that the 'wicked and detestable' Mrs Cummings had enticed Jeannie away.

The second letter stated that he was going to look at the house where she was living in the hope he could 'see her dear face again at the last moment'. His planned suicide he saw as the only thing he could do, having lost 'all that is dear to me'.

At this stage the coroner felt that the jury needed no further evidence, nor did the case require further comment from him. There was only one verdict they could return, and that was that the 'deceased man murdered the deceased woman and afterwards took his own life'. The foreman of the jury stated that they were of the opinion that Jeannie Tait was 'wilfully murdered' by George Facer and that he committed suicide 'whilst in a state of insanity'.

# CHAPTER 16

# Rural Double Murder

Albert and Emma Watson, aged 47 and 50 respectively, had moved from North London to a quiet spot half a mile from Basildon Rectory. Mr Watson had given up his main employment as a carpenter, and their two sons were settled professionally, one as an architect and the other serving as a sailor on HMS *Victory*. Their smallholding was well stocked and tended, providing all their daily needs, and they were regular church-goers, Mr Watson regularly preaching at the Christian Mission Chapel. The only thing they did not have was water, but their neighbour, Mr Buckham of Sawyers Farm in Honeypot Lane, allowed them access to his pond – part of his 26 acres – and this happy arrangement continued for six months.

The summer of 1906 was a hot one, and Mr Buckham had dug out the pond, leaving the water no more than 18 inches deep. He did not look after his land as well as the Watsons, preferring to focus on his engineering job in East London, which meant he had to catch the 6.45am train from Laindon every morning.

Wednesday 23 August started off as just another day. But not for long. At 10am Robert Buckham (16) and his brother Richard (20) ran to the main road and attracted the attention of Thomas Stevens, a local dairy farmer, announcing that two people had drowned in their pond. In the company of several neighbours, Stevens went to investigate the boys' story. He sent his son to fetch the police as soon as he saw the body of Albert Watson lying face down in the water, with his wife's body in a crouching position beside him with blood on her neck, her hands and in the clay all around. Empty pails were upturned near the bodies.

Constable Layzell, on his arrival, supervised the moving of the bodies into the Watsons' bungalow. His sergeant, Richard Giggins, examined the bodies, confirming that the man had a bullet wound in his groin and the woman had three bullet wounds in her chest. A search of the bungalow suggested that there had been an intruder of some description. No weapon was found at this stage, and when Mr Buckham came home from work, he was told by the police that the Watsons had drowned, suggesting suicide. Nevertheless Mr Buckham – and his wife and daughters – were upset at the thought of such a thing happening on their property.

The following morning Superintendent Alfred Marden arrived on the scene, and, on learning that the examining doctor felt the shots had come from behind, questioned the two boys more closely. Marden had a mixed track record in the area – it was he who had been involved in the attempted murder at Sutton a few years earlier and in the unsolved murder of Emma Hunt at Rochford, as well as the more spectacularly successful cases of Florence Dennis and Ann Wilkes. Under his questioning, Robert soon broke down, blaming his brother Richard. When their farm was searched, two guns were found – used primarily to shoot rabbits – and the boys were arrested and both charged with murder on the spot. They had a track record of minor offences, but nothing on this scale.

The boys were conveyed to the local police station in separate vehicles. Richard confessed that he had gone into Mr Watson's house and stolen 4s 6½d and a silver watch. His brother confirmed that he had seen the money and watch but 'did not have any of it'. Superintendent Marden instructed that they be sent on remand to Chelmsford prison.

Once news of the murders broke, the local population took their usual morbid interest in all things gruesome – reminiscent of the rubber-necking often seen today after motorway accidents. They found their way to the remote area by train, motor car, motorcycle, or in carriages, brakes, wagonettes, and even on crutches. One paper mentioned that it was rare to see so many bicycles together in one spot, and there was some reporting of 'souvenirs' being removed from the scene – branches from the oak tree overhanging the pond, pieces of shrubbery with shot embedded and the like.

At the inquest the jury returned a verdict of wilful murder, and the boys were committed to the next Assize which was in November. The younger son, Robert, was acquitted, while the defence for the elder boy concentrated on his mental instability. Richard's father gave evidence that there was insanity in the family, citing a grandfather who had died in a padded cell, a

Superintendent Alfred Marden, the investigating officer. (*Essex Police Museum*)

grandmother with a mania for breaking windows and insulting her friends, who had died 'a raving lunatic', and his own sister's 'uncontrollable fits of passion'. Further evidence of the boy's insanity was found in his high palate, his oddly shaped head, and his habit of tearing his clothes off at mealtimes. However, the judge felt that there was nothing to show that the prisoner was not responsible for his actions.

The jurors, however, were very interested in the motive behind these murders. It seems that Richard Buckham junior had seen himself as head of the household in his father's absence and had told the Watsons they could have no water that day. From this an argument developed, but whether the shots were then meant to frighten the couple or kill them was debatable. In Mrs Watson's case, the gun would have to have been reloaded to fire the third shot. There was also the additional issue that the brothers had entered their victims' home and taken some money and a watch. Could they have been attempting, somewhat clumsily, to cover up their crime?

There was high drama in the court when a couple of notes were produced. Both had been written by Richard, and he was trying to smuggle them to the younger boy when they were both imprisoned. These notes were full of reassurances, but read as confessions, and the wording was, to say the least, unfortunate for the accused. For example, one sentence read 'if you say I said they drove me mad it will be alright'. Young Robert gave the final evidence in the trial, causing quite a stir and helping the jurors make up their minds. He spoke of at least one earlier occasion when Richard had told his brother the Watsons should be shot because they were taking too much water. Although he then back-tracked, saying that 'ought to be shot' did not mean shot by Richard, the damage was done.

In the end the jury was unanimous in announcing a verdict of guilty. In November 1906 a petition was sent to Herbert Gladstone, Secretary of State for Home Affairs, from the Society for the Abolition of Capital Punishment. This letter refers to evidence given by Richard's father about insanity in the family, the prisoner's unreasoning passion (rather than premeditation) and his youth, but no reprieve was forthcoming. Executioner Henry Pierrepoint made a visit to Springfield prison, Chelmsford, in December and Richard was duly hanged.

The funeral at Great Burstead Church was crowded with mourners. Eventually Honeypot Lane disappeared as the new town of Basildon developed after the Second World War. As for Robert, he joined the 1st Royal Dragoons and had attained the rank of sergeant by the end of the First World War, receiving the Military Medal in 1917.

Interestingly, this case, where the police investigations took place in one of the most inaccessible districts of Essex, prompted a campaign for the police force to purchase cars for official use – which was in the end, of course, successful.

For a scrupulously documented and detailed account of this case, interested parties should refer to *The Honeypot Killers* by Marion Hill, published by Next Century Books.

The funeral of the Watsons. (*Essex Police Museum*)

# CHAPTER 17

# Holiday Murders

The date: Monday 13 February 1922. The location: the Victoria Restaurant, 19 Eastern Esplanade, Southend. The discovery: a man trying to murder a woman in an upstairs room.

The restaurant's proprietor, Albert Wittleton, gave a graphic account of the incident to a *Southend Standard* reporter soon afterwards. A respectable couple, George Pearce of south-east London and his wife, had booked a room a few days earlier. They had checked out after a few days, apparently on the best of terms, and had been seen walking along Marine Parade at 10am on that fateful Monday morning. Soon after, they reappeared at the Victoria unexpectedly, asking if they could use the empty room again 'for a few minutes'. Mr Wittleton was happy enough to agree.

His happiness did not last, however, because soon afterwards he heard a woman screaming, together with noises that sounded like furniture being thrown about and broken. Mr Wittleton rushed up the stairs, found the door to their room open, and saw the woman lying on her back on the floor with the man astride her, slashing at her with a razor. She was, naturally, struggling and screaming, and Mr Wittleton managed to pull the man off. George Pearce made no attempt to run away. In the meantime Wittleton had called for someone to get the police, and he then assisted the woman downstairs to find some help for her, she having been cut about the face, neck and arm, with part of an ear severed.

When PC Mallett arrived, Wittleton took him to the upstairs room where Pearce was lying on the bed, partly covered with clothing. Pearce then managed to say a few words to the police officer: 'It's all right, policeman. I have taken poison.' The room was pervaded with the smell of carbolic, and PC Mallett asked Wittleton to mix an emetic and send for Dr Lloyd. Although there was only a minimal delay before the doctor's arrival – only enough time to administer the emetic, but to no effect – there had been little hope and the man died soon afterwards.

On being asked for his opinion, Wittleton could not 'imagine what possessed' Pearce, only that he must have had some kind of 'sudden fit'. A small square bottle which had contained poison was found in the room, which was at the top of several flights of narrow stairs. The missing ear-lobe was found in the room when it was searched by PC Gray. The reporter gained access to this room and described it as having a 'blood-spattered' wardrobe and bed with obvious signs of a struggle, a chair and towel rail having been broken.

The same evening, with her head and right hand bandaged, the woman was escorted by PC Gray from hospital to the police station in Alexandra Street. There she made a statement, giving her name as Alice Vincent from south-east London, and confirming that the dead man's name was George Pearce. He lived at a neighbouring address.

At the inquest a few days later at the Park Hotel, Dr Lloyd was the first to give evidence. Pearce was already unconscious when he arrived on the scene, and there was nothing to be done. The symptoms – the white, hard lips and gums – were of carbolic acid poisoning, borne out by the strong smell in the room. When shown the brown bottle, the witness felt that it had undoubtedly contained the poison.

Alfred Pearce had already identified the body as that of his brother, a bachelor aged 37. Alfred declared himself to be a railway ticket collector from Bermondsey in London, and told the coroner that his brother had been a postman until being dismissed recently on suspicion of theft. George, who had served during the First World War in the Artillery and then the Royal Engineers, had absolutely denied any wrong-doing and the accusation had really upset him. Indeed, he was so upset that he had written a letter to Alfred, which was produced in court, saying that:

*I am fed up and absolutely broken through the circumstances. I am going right away and shall poison myself. I shall try to keep my identity hidden. I am sorry to have to leave this world, but in the circumstances, with my character taken away and being damaged without the slightest chance of getting a job, it is more than I can stand. It is a far, far better thing that I do now than I have ever done – it is the only way. I send my love to you and Sid and I hope poor dear mother will never learn of my fate.*

A final letter, dated 13 February and posted in Southend, was also produced in court, wherein George stated that 'this last affair' was more than he could bear, and protested again his absolute innocence. His biggest worry was obviously his lack of prospects of getting any further work. Concluding his evidence, Alfred also mentioned that George had drawn all of his savings after demobilisation – more than £300 – which he had spent on various women, Alice Vincent being one of them. Only 18s was found in his pocket after his death.

Alice, still swathed in bandages, told the deputy coroner that she was in domestic service, she was aged 24 and she was a spinster. She had known George Pearce for about eighteen months and had been away with him several times, including weekends at Brighton and Southend, occupying the same room. They had met up for their Southend weekend at Borough station in London and booked a room over the Victoria Restaurant until the Monday morning. Pearce had been quieter than usual, having recently lost his job, which was obviously worrying him, but he had been his usual 'kind' self. She admitted that he had been drinking heavily, however, on Sunday night, downing double whiskies.

On their final morning they had breakfast at the Victoria and went to the GER station at Southend to ask about trains back to London. Before leaving, Pearce had shown her the brown bottle and told her it was whisky, before putting it into his mackintosh pocket.

The weather being unseasonably warm, the couple had made leisurely stops at a couple of different pubs, drinking a Guinness stout in each and had established that they would return to London on the 4.30 train. As they had some time left, they returned to the Victoria, and George followed her up to the upstairs room, suddenly producing a razor from his pocket. She had never seen it before as he was in the habit of shaving 'at the barber's shop'. After placing the razor and the brown bottle on the washstand he removed his mackintosh and jacket and asked Alice how much money she had.

When she said she had 7 shillings, it seems Pearce wanted to check her bag but Alice refused to let him. Pearce then blocked her exit and asked for a kiss. After they had embraced, she had felt – from the look on his face – that something was wrong and asked him to let her go by, but that was when he had punched her to the ground and picked up the razor. She managed to grab the razor from him, but he then struck her with the towel rail.

When he managed to retrieve the razor, he slashed her from her mouth to the back of her neck, and cut off part of her ear.

Pearce's behaviour towards Alice was perhaps the most baffling part of this case. However, this was not something that the jury members needed to concern themselves with. In his address to the jury, the coroner said that 'the facts were plain, and all they had to consider was the question of the state of the man's mind'. As a result, the jurors were unanimous in declaring that the deceased had committed suicide during temporary insanity following his assault on Alice Vincent.

★★★★

AND JUST A FEW WEEKS LATER . . .

The date: the early hours of Thursday 2 March 1922. The location: the water's edge on the beach, Marine Parade, Southend. The discovery: a woman's body, spotted by PC Reenan on his regular patrol. She was alive, but unconscious and soaked through. PC Reenan managed to revive her by the time his sergeant arrived on the scene. Her first words, upon seeing the police officer, were: 'Is that you, sweetheart?' Sergeant Drage, seeing her confusion, asked if she had taken anything and she admitted to drinking not only port wine but also a tonic called Easton's syrup (which was known to contain strychnine) and some tablets. However, a quick search for her hat on the beach revealed something even more sinister – another body, this time of a man, floating on the water.

The sergeant started artificial respiration on the man, while Reenan ran for assistance. He found a night watchman and took the woman to his hut so that she could be given an emetic, while Drage continued to try to save the man's life, but to no effect. The woman was removed to the Victoria Hospital and the body to the mortuary.

The woman identified herself as Mary Baker from Mile End Road in East London, and Sergeant Drage visited her in order to advise her that attempting suicide was a criminal offence. At this point she admitted that she and Jack Palmer had mutually agreed to end it all when their money had run out the previous weekend. Jack had provided the tablets and they had both taken the syrup and drunk the wine. As a result of this explanation, Chief Inspector Crockford visited Mary in hospital the next morning, explaining that he was arresting her on a charge of wilful murder of John Thomas Hilton Palmer, because the

Marine Parade, Southend. The boating lake has since been replaced by an amusement park. (*Author's Collection*)

survivor of a suicide pact was, in law, thus guilty of murder.

Upon her release from hospital, Mary was formally charged. By now she had veered away from the suicide pact story and made out instead that she had been coerced into it by Jack. She now explained that she had taken the wine and syrup because she did not know what she was doing.

The next day's inquest at the Park Hotel was reported in the *Southend Standard*. The story of the relationship between John Palmer and Mary was revealed in court. He had been married since 1911, but had been separated since 1919. Mrs Palmer, who had identified her husband's body, appeared in court but was not happy about revealing the circumstances of their separation, although she did confirm that her husband saw his three children regularly at their address in East London. Recently he had been staying with his married sister in Clapton, also in East London, and his maintenance payments had slipped only after his mother had died and he had been ill, spending some time in hospital and being unable to work regularly at his job with Kodak. When asked if her husband was a man who liked a drink, Mrs Palmer said she did not think he had been drinking since coming out of hospital, and she denied that drink was a factor in their separation.

It transpired, according to Mrs Palmer, that Mary Baker had been a regular visitor at the Clapton house because her 'sweetheart' lodged there – in fact it was this 'sweetheart' who had introduced her to Jack. She was friendly with the Palmer children and Mrs Palmer had never realised her involvement with Jack. In fact, there had been recent talk of a reconciliation between husband and wife.

Additional witnesses gave evidence although Mary was not in court. Dr Walker confirmed that he had carried out a post-mortem examination on the deceased, which revealed a 'fatty degeneration of the heart'. Palmer had a blackened tongue and the stomach was congested, the latter organ having been sealed and preserved. In his view, death had been a result of asphyxiation, possibly accelerated by his heart condition, but he could not say whether poisoning had also accelerated his death. Two tubes of photographic tabloids were produced in court, having been found on the beach by one of the many 'tourists' who had been haunting Marine Parade since Mr Palmer's death. There were indeed some tablets missing from the tubes, presumably obtained from Palmer's employers, and although the doctor felt that the contents could have been responsible for the blackened tongues of both Palmer and Baker, he did not feel qualified to comment on how deadly these tablets might have been.

Sergeant Drage and PC Reenan gave accounts of their involvement, revealing that John Palmer had only a penny in his pocket, along with some letters identified as being from Miss Baker. A gold wedding ring was found in the nearby shelter, apparently bought for Mary by her lover but left behind deliberately as she did not want to be found wearing it. An empty port wine bottle was also found in the shelter, showing how the couple had spent their time while waiting for the tide to come in before they could carry out their planned actions.

Mrs Roper, the landlady at 14 Grover Street, Southend, spoke up about the couple – married as far as she was aware – who had been staying with her since the previous Saturday. They had paid 33 shillings in advance for their room, enough for one week, but on the last day, Tuesday, Mary had told her that she was trying to persuade the deceased to stay another night. They returned for one more evening, with Palmer reportedly 'fuddled' by drink. In fact, Mrs Roper gave evidence that she had cleared four empty port wine bottles out of their room on Monday morning and another six on Wednesday morning.

The jury was reconvened the following Thursday, and the coroner reminded the jurors that if they decided to return a verdict of suicide in regard to the man, they were at liberty to consider the question as to the condition of his mind at the time, as well as the effects of the alcohol. The jury returned a verdict of suicide during temporary insanity. Mr Lewis also commended the actions of the police, especially in administering the emetic to the woman, resulting in her vomiting, without which she too would have been likely to die.

The next day Mary Baker stood trial for the 'wilful murder with malice aforethought' of Jack Palmer, with the additional charge of attempted suicide. Justice J.W. Burrows presided. Mrs Palmer, dressed in black, sat at the back of the court in tears. Inspector Crockford said he would offer no evidence in regard to the murder charge as statements showed that the man was probably the instigator of the whole affair. He would leave the Bench to deal with the case of attempted suicide.

Mary had nothing to add, but her father was in court. James Thomas Baker, a packer, had reported his daughter missing on Monday morning when she had not returned from a weekend visit to 'see a friend'. He had heard nothing after that until receiving the telegram sent by the police at Southend on Thursday to say Mary was in hospital. On being questioned as to whether he felt able to look after Mary if she should return home, he agreed, if a little reluctantly, that he would do so 'to the best of his ability'. The prisoner confirmed that she wished to return to the family home, so the Chairman announced he had no desire to prolong the agony she must be suffering and sent her home under a probation order into the care of her father for a period of twelve months for the attempted suicide. The murder charge was dropped.

Southend police had had a busy month.

CHAPTER 18

# The McIlroy Mystery

As PC Abbott was passing Sidney Bartlett's drapers in Hamlet Court Road on his beat in the early hours of a Saturday morning in 1934, he heard a sound from inside and saw the flash of a torch. On investigating the rear entrance, he saw a parked taxi-cab, the driver of which explained that he was waiting for a fare booked for that spot at one o'clock. PC Abbott instead told the driver to take him 'as fast as he could' to Westcliff police station, on the corner of West and Claremont Roads, to collect reinforcements.

When the police returned, they could make out a couple of figures moving around inside the shop. They were joined by PC Roper, who had run all the way from the police box in Holland Road, but they were thinly stretched to cover the various exits from the shop, a substantial double-fronted building. While another police officer, PC Lawrence, was talking to the taxi driver, a man dashed from the passage alongside the drapers, bleeding from the face, and a struggle commenced as PC Lawrence waylaid him. The policeman was trying to manhandle the man into the taxi when the man fired a revolver, singeing the officer's knuckles but luckily doing no further damage. PC Roper drew his truncheon and struck the man on the head but he still managed to break free, crossing and recrossing the London Road and escaping into Ceylon Road, with the police in pursuit.

The taxi driver was again called into service to search the area, but to no avail, and he was then allowed to return to his normal duties. Later, however, Detective Sergeant Moss and PC Lawrence went to question the driver, Leslie Gordon Whyte, at his home in Northview Drive, about the mysterious fare he had been waiting for. During this visit PC Lawrence spotted a photograph of a man hanging on the wall of the dining-room, whom he recognised as the man who had shot at him. This man turned out to be Roy McIlroy, aged 23, a bachelor who lived

The site of Bartlett's in Hamlet Court Road, 2007. (*Author*)

with his widowed mother at the same Northview Drive address, and was Whyte's partner in a motor-car business. As a result, Whyte was taken to the police station, where he was charged at 3.30am with conspiring with McIlroy to break into Bartlett's. That same morning officers had found a quantity of brown paper and treacle on the premises, a combination often used by shop-breakers to break glass noiselessly, and had ascertained that entry into the main shop had been gained by climbing the iron grille in front of the premises and forcing a showcase window. They had also managed to establish that a total of 33*s* in coins had been stolen. A broken window was discovered at the rear, marked with blood, which was presumed to indicate McIlroy's exit route.

In the meantime, retired farmer Mr Reynolds and his wife of Elderton Road were disturbed by their dog barking at around 1am. They heard a man's voice call out 'I'm running away' on being challenged, before hearing what sounded like a shot. They assumed the man had shot at their dog, so they went to check on the animal. He was not harmed, although he continued whining through the night. When Mr Reynolds went out of his back door at 8 in the morning he found a shocking sight: the body of a dead man was huddled in a narrow pathway at the side of his home, his legs partly outstretched in front of him, his head and shoulders sagging forward, and with a large bullet wound to his forehead. There was a lot of blood. Mr Reynolds called the police. Roy McIlroy had been found.

The *Southend Standard* of 1 February reported that 'death had been instantaneous', with 'considerable singeing showing that the shot had been fired at close quarters'. Most of the blood at the scene was McIlroy's, from the wounds he had suffered when smashing his way out of the window of Bartlett's. There was also a report of an abrasion on the skull, possibly caused by PC Roper's truncheon. The first finger of the dead man's right hand was round the trigger of a Browning automatic revolver from which two bullets had been fired. The body was removed to the mortuary.

A special Police Court was convened later the same day, Saturday, to charge Whyte. He had already heard that McIlroy was dead and had made a statement to the police to the effect that he had seen McIlroy struggling with PC Lawrence when a shot was fired. It seems that the further content of Whyte's statement resulted in another arrest the same day, because Ernest Leonard Horsfall, aged 25, a bus conductor from Park Lane, Southend, appeared at the Police Court on the following Monday, also charged with breaking, entering and theft. Several uniformed drivers and conductors of the Westcliff Motor Service were in the public seats at the court. Horsfall, admitting his presence at the crime scene, claimed that he hadn't even known McIlroy had a gun until he heard the shot, by which time he (Horsfall) was already 'well away'.

The inquest on McIlroy was held by the Borough Coroner

the next day, Tuesday. One of the witnesses was the deceased man's sister Phyllis, who was so distressed that her evidence was barely audible. It seems that she and her mother had known that McIlroy had a revolver but had been urging him to get rid of it because he didn't have a licence. He had picked it up in Paris when he worked there some years earlier. It seems that Whyte also had a revolver. Phyllis left the court in tears shortly afterwards after hearing about her brother's struggle with PC Lawrence. She would no doubt have been even more upset if she had heard the graphic evidence then supplied by Dr Hiscocks, who had carried out the post-mortem on McIlroy, in the course of which his brain was removed. Dr Hiscocks confirmed that the wound was self-inflicted, and that death was caused by a gunshot fired into the brain and had nothing to do with the abrasion on his head 'caused by a blunt instrument'.

There were several further witnesses. Mr Ernest Harvey, a garage proprietor from Inverness Avenue, gave evidence of identification, McIlroy having been known to him for some twelve months. Mr Reynolds told how he had heard the man at the back of his house in the early hours, not realising what was happening, and how he had found the body the next morning. Inspector Fletcher had been the one to check out Mr Reynolds' discovery and, on being questioned by a juror, explained that McIlroy would have had to climb two fences to end up where he did – so perhaps it was no wonder the police officers had not been able to find him in the dark. The police officers involved reprised the events of the break-in.

While there was no doubt about the cause of McIlroy's death, there was the question of why he had shot himself. There was no evidence of any mental instability according to Mr Harvey or Miss McIlroy, and the latter did not think he had any financial problems. The only reasonable explanation was that he thought he had inflicted a more serious injury on PC Lawrence than was actually the case. In which case, being *compos mentis*, he had killed himself deliberately and the coroner advised the jury to say so. The foreman felt that McIlroy 'knew quite well what he was doing', and the coroner believed that the verdict of *felo de se* was the right one. He also congratulated the police officers on the way they had handled the situation and on their lucky escape from more serious injury. If McIlroy had known that PC Lawrence had suffered only burned knuckles, would he still have taken his own life? We shall never know.

# CHAPTER 19

# Arson, Poison, and a Cut Throat

The firemen of Leigh Fire Brigade were involved in an interesting exercise on 19 April 1938. Called out to a fire in Nelson Drive, Leigh-on-Sea, they arrived to see smoke issuing from the front upstairs room over the antique shop. They had some trouble gaining access to the premises as the front door of the shop was bolted and barred and a table had been pushed up against it. Once inside, they put out another fire they found in the hall and dashed upstairs, where they could hear a noise in the bathroom. Upon investigating, Officer Harry Emery of Leigh Hill found Edgar William Allen, aged 62, sitting there with a wound to his throat, and he hurriedly secured assistance to move the semi-conscious man down the stairs, enabling the police to take over.

In the meantime the firemen had put out at least four separate fires on the premises, although there was more smoke than fire owing to the smouldering stuffing from broken furniture strewn around the premises. It seemed that the fires had been set up to form a chain, although no petrol or paraffin was thought to have been used. Inspector Moss of the Borough Constabulary, based at Leigh, arrived as Mr Allen was being carried down the stairs. He found a green bottle lying on the kitchen table with its cork removed, and an open case containing a razor next to the spot where Mr Allen had been found.

Mr Allen was taken to Southend Municipal Hospital at Rochford, where he was examined by Dr Cleman. The cut on his throat was only skin deep, and had not put him in any danger. However, he was still semi-conscious, and his breath smelt strongly of camphorated oil. The doctor ordered a stomach wash. The poison had brought on a recurrent bronchial condition, but Mr Allen agreed to be interviewed by Detective Sergeant Hemson on 22 April. It appeared that he had been in some arrears with his rent, and his landlord, although using a lawful means of seizing goods in lieu of the

Leigh police station, dating back to 1911. (*Author*)

debt, wanted more than his entitlement. Allen told the detective that he had been a reliable tenant for over twelve years, but the tenancy agreement should not be broken by either party, and the landlord, Mr Grant, had not always kept his side of the agreement. The last straw came when the bailiffs arrived shortly before Good Friday to make an inventory of the furniture on the premises, even though Mrs Allen had gone to see Mr Grant to appeal for more time to pay. Allen, who lived in a flat above

Southend Municipal Hospital, Rochford, in the 1930s.
(*Southend University Hospital*)

the shop, had managed to keep the bailiffs at bay, and was so determined that Grant would not get his furniture that he admitted setting fire to the premises. However, although admitting arson, Allen said he was too upset to remember if he had tried to cut his throat, and 'could not recall' if he had taken any poison.

Mr Allen's bronchitis – aggravated by the poison he had taken – developed into bronchial pneumonia, and he died on Saturday 30 April. The inquest at Rochford a few days later threw up some interesting developments.

As well as the professionals who had been concerned with Mr Allen's last few days, his housekeeper, Mrs Phoebe Simpson, was also called to give evidence. She looked after the antique and needlework business at Nelson Drive while Mr Allen went to work in the City of London, and had been doing so for over twelve years. It was the Stock Exchange that provided Mr Allen's main income, the shop being more of a hobby. She was aware, however, that he had accumulated some £70 in rent arrears and that Mr Allen was very upset at the imminent arrival of the bailiffs.

On 19 April she had received a telegram which she presumed had been sent by her son Sidney, asking her to go straight to his home at Wembley. But when she got there, her son knew nothing about the telegram, and she returned the

Leigh-on-Sea, before the Second World War. (*Author's Collection*)

following morning to find that Mr Allen was in hospital. The next day she had received a letter from her employer emphasising his financial difficulties and his inability to see a way out of the mess. Her son also gave evidence, denying all knowledge of the telegram. Mrs Simpson agreed with the coroner's suggestion that the telegram had been sent to get her out of the way, and that the letter was by way of a farewell.

Mr Beccle, the coroner, also questioned the deceased's brother Frank Allen, a company director, who had travelled up from Kent. Frank Allen could only confirm that his brother was some kind of financial agent and antique dealer, but said he was a reserved man who had revealed nothing of his difficulties. The first thing the witness had known about the events was when he saw a newspaper report.

However, it was a sentence spoken by the deceased to Detective Sergeant Hemson at the hospital which made the most impact on the coroner. Mr Allen could not remember attempting suicide, but had said at the close of the interview: 'I was so upset, my mental balance went astray.' In response to this, Mr Beccle said: 'I think everything is contained in that last sentence.' He returned a verdict of suicide while the balance of his mind was disturbed, and added that the situation would have been a great shock for someone of Allen's age, sufficient to 'unbalance' him.

# CHAPTER 20

# Patricide in Rayleigh

In the summer of 1943 war news still pervaded the local press. South-east Essex was still being targeted by German air raids, and bombs were causing considerable damage in the area. One explosion turned out to have a rather different origin, however.

On Friday 23 July, a seasonably sunny day, Nurse Elsie Mitchell was surprised to find the air raid shelter housing her patient's wheelchair locked. She had to ask the patient's wife to help her, and the two of them were more than a little surprised to find inside, when the door was suddenly opened, the son of the house. Eric Brown was on compassionate leave from his army posting at Spilsby in Lincolnshire, his mother having requested his assistance in coping with her invalid husband Archibald at their home in London Hill, Rayleigh.

Archibald Brown, then aged 47, had been seriously injured in a motorcycle accident over twenty years earlier, but in 1938 spinal paralysis had resulted in him losing the use of his legs. This long spell of incapacity had turned Mr Brown into a bitter individual, who verbally abused his wife Dorothy constantly, and repeatedly humiliated both her and their eldest son Eric. His demands became overwhelming and wholly unreasonable. Eric had escaped some of his father's influence when he was sent away to boarding school, while the younger son Colin seems to have avoided the worst of his father's excesses. By joining the army Eric had hoped to avoid any further contact with his father, so he was not best pleased that his mother had arranged for him to have extra leave.

What happened next ended a life of tyranny for Dorothy Brown and her 19-year-old son. Nurse Mitchell had settled Mr Brown in his wheelchair, he had lit the cigarette he relished on these occasions, and she was pushing him past Rayleigh Church when there was a huge explosion. The nurse collapsed with terrible leg injuries, but her life had been saved by the cushion

The remains of Archibald Brown's wheelchair. (*Essex Police Museum*)

and pillows between her and the explosive's source. Mr Brown, however, had been blown to pieces, quite literally. One leg was found in a tree some 30 feet away, the other had landed in a front garden 48 feet away, and his bloodied torso was lying in the road, with other parts of his dismembered body spread around the vicinity. The force of the explosion had blown out nearby windows, and all that remained of the invalid chair was a mass of twisted metal.

The initial reaction, as reported by the excitable local press, was that Brown had been killed either by a low-flying aircraft or as the result of his wheelchair hitting an unexploded bomb. But by the time Dr Gilmour had carried out his post-mortem the next day, it was becoming clear that the explosive device used had actually been attached to the wheelchair – or to Mr Brown himself. Explosive experts were called in and identified the source of the explosion as a British anti-tank mine, a Hawkins grenade, which seemed to have been secreted under the wheelchair's cushion. In other words, the police had a murder on their hands. At this point the investigation was put into the hands of Detective Superintendent George 'Tot' Totterdell, the head of Essex CID.

Interviewing Mrs Brown revealed little. She had never seen either son with any explosive, nor did she know what a grenade looked like. While admitting that Eric had made remarks to her along the lines of 'I wonder how you stick it' when discussing his father's obnoxious behaviour, they had been on better terms in recent years. Totterdell decided to investigate further. There had been a few strange transactions at the bank in Rochford where Eric worked after leaving school, involving unauthorised cheques and missing cash, and these anomalies had resulted in him being asked to resign. Then, on checking the records of Eric's Suffolk Regiment, it was revealed that Eric had attended lectures on the very mine used to kill his father, and had access to a store of some two hundred mines at Spilsby, some of which were used for training with no check kept on them. Eric also had ample opportunity to study the manuals describing the mechanism of these particular mines. Some experiments were then made with an identical chair, the police concluding that the explosion had been triggered when Mr Brown shifted his weight after lighting his cigarette.

Not unnaturally, Eric was interviewed soon after at Rayleigh police station, in view of the fact that he had the means and opportunity to kill his father. He was asked to account for his presence in the air raid shelter just before the explosion. Initially, in the company of three detectives, Eric, a boyish bespectacled youth, had proved reluctant to provide any information at all. However, when left alone with the experienced Totterdell, he had finally agreed to make a voluntary statement. He explained that he wanted to put both his father and mother out of their 'suffering' after seeing how much of an unhappy drudge his mother had become in the family home. This was the motive the police had been looking for. As a result, Eric was arrested and charged with murder. He made two appearances at Southend Petty Sessional Court, represented by Mr J.P. Nolan, with Mr J.F. Claxton acting for the Crown. Sergeant Smith, the battalion weapons instructor, told the court that Private Brown 'probably' attended his lectures on British mines, but he could not swear that he had done so. Dr Gilmour, Eric's commanding officer Captain Bell, several explosives experts, the policeman who had attended the scene of the explosion and the detectives who had interrogated Brown all gave evidence supporting Mr Claxton's case. Mr Nolan, however, was not happy with the statement that Brown had given, suggesting that it had been made only after it had been suggested to his client that his mother could suffer in some way if he did not 'come clean'. This was vehemently denied and the Bench ruled that the confession, for such it was, could be read out in court. As a result, Eric Brown was committed for trial at Essex Assizes in November.

Mrs Brown then felt able to come forward to give more information about her husband's treatment of her and Eric. It seems that he had tipped tea over her, rung a bell to summon her constantly, grabbed her clothes to pull her down, and had once attempted to strangle her. As for Eric, he had been persist- ently bullied by his father when he was at school locally, at Rayleigh Grammar. Mr Brown had often struck him on the head or across the face for no apparent reason, had locked him in a dark cupboard under the stairs or in the shed, or sent him to bed early. It seems that Mrs Brown had often thought of leaving her unpleasant husband, and even had a suitcase packed ready, but had never got that far.

The trial of Private Eric James Brown on 4 November at Shire Hall, Chelmsford, lasted only one day. He pleaded not guilty but the defending counsel, Mr Cecil Havers, made no attempt to deny that his client had indeed murdered Archibald Brown. He concentrated on Brown's state of mind instead: had he known what he was doing? He called as a witness Dr Rowland Hill, the psychiatrist who had examined the prisoner, who suggested that Brown could be in the early stages of schizo-phrenia. However, the medical officer of Chelmsford prison, Dr R.G. Lyster, called by Sir Charles Doughty for the prosecution, said that the only indication that Brown had shown of any form of insanity had been an attempt at suicide in October when he cut his neck with a knife. Finally Detective Inspector Barkway, who had been investigating Eric's antecedents, said he had established that there was 'insanity' in the Brown family, affecting some grandparents and an aunt.

Mr Justice Atkinson was clearly not convinced, because in his summing up he remarked that he felt Eric Brown knew 'very well' what he was doing. However, the jury came to the conclusion that the weight of evidence, together with the incident at Barclays Bank and Eric's generally erratic behaviour – no doubt aggravated by his father – were enough to regard him as irrational. After just 45 minutes' deliberation their verdict was 'guilty but insane' and Mr Justice Atkinson ordered that Eric be detained in custody 'as a criminal lunatic'. And detained he certainly was, only being released some thirty-two years later.

# CHAPTER 21

# Double Murder in Leigh-on-Sea

va Rosemary Lucas, aged 17, made a horrifying discovery on Wednesday 6 June 1945 when she arrived home after a day's work at her hairdressing job in East London. Life for the Lucases was beginning to return to some sort of normality following the VE day celebrations the month before. It was Eva's usual time, around 6.40pm, but all the doors of the home she shared with her parents in Undercliff Gardens, Leigh, were locked. Nor was there any trace of the family's black cocker spaniel. Eva forced a way in through a casement window into her mother's bedroom at the front of the bungalow, and then went on into the hall, where she found her mother lying on her back, covered with an eiderdown and with a coat over her head.

Eva's first reaction was to reach out for her mother's arm, which was cold to the touch. At this, she left the house by the front door and sent a passing woman to fetch the police, returning almost immediately with the postman – who had just arrived – to investigate further. Noticing the open dining-room door, Eva went in and saw her father lying on the floor covered by a carpet and with a cushion over his head.

Given the condition of the premises, with broken furniture and crockery in the dining room and large amounts of blood on the walls and ceiling, the first police officer on the scene, Inspector Percy Moss from Leigh, was in no doubt that a savage double murder had taken place. Police surgeon Dr Newman Norman, of King's Road, Westcliff, attended the bungalow the same evening, confirming the suspicions of the police, and expert officers from the Criminal Investigation Department of New Scotland Yard were called upon to take charge of the case. The Metropolitan and Southend forces worked together and promptly made an arrest. John Riley Young, aged about 40, from Ilford, was charged with murder on Saturday 9 June.

Leigh-on-Sea in about 1940, close to the murder scene. (*Author's Collection*)

A special court was convened at Southend that afternoon, presided over by Mayor (Alderman) Miles, with Young in the dock between two policemen. The accused was described in the *Southend Standard* of 14 June as 'stockily built and dark complexioned . . . dressed in a well cut brown pin-striped suit with a light brown open-necked shirt'; he looked tired and haggard, with his wrists bandaged, his eyes bloodshot and his forehead bruised. The only word he spoke in court was a mumbled 'Yes' when asked if he needed legal aid. The Chief Constable of Southend commented that at this stage of the proceedings he was only calling evidence of the arrest, and needed time to collect other evidence while the prisoner was held on remand.

It fell to Detective Inspector Harris to confirm that Young had been detained at East Ham police station in East London that morning, and conveyed to Southend to be charged with the murders. Young – who had been treated the day before in Oldchurch Hospital, Romford, for cut wrists – responded only by expressing sorrow about what had happened, repeatedly saying that he 'did not know' how it had happened. He was granted legal aid and remanded until the following Friday, and his defence was put in the hands of Mr Henry Flint, a Southend solicitor.

In Southend on the following Tuesday Eva Lucas gave her disturbing evidence at the inquest, in the presence of the Borough Coroner, Mr H.J. Jefferies, and a jury of eight men. The *Southend Standard* gave an account of the occasion, a deeply unpleasant one for such a young girl who had already had to formally identify the bodies of her parents, Frederick and Cissie Lucas, both aged 52. Eva was dressed in a 'blue and black check coat' with a black mourning band on her left arm. She arrived in court accompanied by her sister Doreen, a sergeant in the ATS, and her brother-in-law, Regimental Sergeant-Major Thraves. She bravely described the harrowing discoveries she had made, and subsequently explained that she herself worked as a hairdresser in Leytonstone, East London, and that her father had been a jeweller. They had moved to Leigh from London in May and had been looking forward to a more peaceful and optimistic future in new surroundings.

Dr Norman also gave evidence at the inquest. He had assisted with the post-mortem examination, which was carried out on 7 June at Southend mortuary by Dr Simpson, a Home Office pathologist. He felt that Mr Lucas was of generally good physique and health. He had suffered severe injuries to his head, probably caused by a blunt instrument. Dr Norman felt that he must have received at least six blows of considerable violence. The blows were probably inflicted while his head was erect, in a standing or sitting position, but there was another blow on the left side of his face which could have been made while he was lying on the floor. The little finger of his left hand was broken. His brain was 'lacerated' and the skull fractured. The trunk of his body was free from injury, with the exception of slight bruising. Death, in the witness's opinion, was due to shock from the injuries.

As regards Mrs Lucas, the doctor said that she, too, was of a healthy physique. Her injuries were at the back of the head and on the left side of the face and cheek. They were also probably caused by a blunt instrument. It seemed that she might have been attacked from behind, resulting in a fractured skull and a 'contused' brain. The blood from the facial injuries had run into her throat, flooding the air passages and no doubt hastening her death, which the doctor attributed to asphyxia and shock. The couple had obviously been the victims of an exceptionally violent attack. Only their dog had escaped. It was found in Barking a few days later and brought back to Eva.

John Young made a second brief appearance before Southend Magistrates on Friday 15 June. The case had already been referred to the Director of Public Prosecutions, and the prosecution would be prepared for the case from 6 July, requiring a further period of remand, which was granted by the Chairman, Mr H.H. Burrows, with no protest from Young or his defending solicitor. In the meantime the Lucases had been buried at Woodgrange Park, and Sergeant Doreen Thraves had applied for a discharge from the forces so that she could move to the Southend area to be near her sister.

The July Police Court proceedings were opened on behalf of the Director of Public Prosecutions by Mr H.J. Parham. He first described Young as a builder, who had done some business with Mr Lucas in connection with the sale of some sovereigns. He then moved on to the timing of the two murders, which was established as taking place at around 9am: Mr Lucas's wristwatch had stopped at that time, having obviously had a knock. This timing apparently confirmed the medical evidence.

Parham talked about Young's movements on that fateful day, 6 June. He had left his home in Ilford at around 7am for a pre-arranged meeting with Mr Lucas at 8.30, and had returned at around 2pm. He was seen in Undercliff Gardens by the woman living next door to the Lucases, who had a conversation with him around 10am. The next day he had phoned his landlady around 10pm and she told him the police had been looking for him. As a result, he did not return to his lodgings but went to stay with his sister in Barking. At his sister's home, he tried first to gas himself and then, when that failed, he slit his wrists and had to be treated at Oldchurch Hospital at Romford. A form of will was found in his pocket at the hospital, wherein he left all his possessions to 'the finest and best little woman in the world', his landlady, Mrs Orford. On the opposite page he had written: 'Goodbye everybody. It is better this way.' Also in his pockets were a business card from Mr Lucas and £140 in cash.

Several police officers, including Chief Inspector Philpott of New Scotland Yard, visited Young in hospital at 9am on Friday 9 June. He wished to confess, and, after being dressed, was taken to the police station, where he made a statement. As a result of this statement, Mr Parham explained that a police officer was sent to Mr Young's business premises where he found a large cache of £5 notes, a gold cigarette case, a leather wallet, twenty-one rings, six packets of precious stones, two pocket watches and two wristwatches, some of which could be identified as belonging to Mr Lucas.

Mr Parham also gave an account of how Mr Young's clothing was examined and found to be extensively blood-stained, including his shoes. Strands of his hair were found on the shirt and cuff-link of the deceased, and a button found at the crime scene seemed to have been ripped from Young's clothing. Further evidence concerned a heel print found at Undercliff Gardens, which matched the rubber heel on the shoes of the accused. (It is interesting to note the forensic progress being made here.)

The first witness called was PC Bonnett of the Southend police who submitted plans of the bungalow and its surroundings. Detective Inspector Law of New Scotland Yard then submitted photographs of the bodies, the crime scene and the imprint of the rubber heel in blood on the dining-room carpet.

Poor Eva Lucas now had to relive her ordeal. She first confirmed that her father always carried jewellery and sums of money about with him, and travelled to many different parts of the country from his Clerkenwell (London) base, sometimes staying away for several days on business. As usual, when she had left for work on the fateful day he was still in bed and her mother was preparing breakfast.

She described once more her horrifying discoveries, but was able to add just one detail. After the doctor and police had left the scene later that evening, she had been sitting on the steps by the front door when she found a red stone, which she believed came from a ring belonging to her father.

Mr Flint, defending, asked Miss Lucas if she could identify the prisoner. At first she refused to look at Young, but, on being directed to do so, was unable to identify him as her father 'had so many friends'.

Next to give evidence was Mrs Ivy Moore, whose husband worked in partnership with Young, operating as Moore & Young (Builders) of High Road, Ilford, Essex. She had known Young for four years, and they were on friendly terms. On Sunday 3 June he had offered to drive her and her little girl to Leigh in his saloon car as he needed to visit Mr Lucas in Undercliff Gardens. They had waited in the car while Young had gone into the bungalow for half an hour. When he came back, the pockets of his sports jacket were bulging, and he explained that he had been trading sovereigns with Mr Lucas for £5 10*s* per sovereign. She had not seen Young since he had dropped them home that evening, but she gave an account of a 'very kindly man'.

The next day, 4 June, Young had called on Mrs Ann Watmough, a garage proprietor from Ilford, and it was her turn to take the oath. She, too, had known him for four or five years, and described him as 'a perfect gentleman . . . docile and kindly'. Young had wanted to hire a car for the next day but none was available until Wednesday, which he had settled for. While there, he had asked if he could place some money in her safe as he did not have anywhere secure to keep it for the time being. Mrs Watmough had agreed 'to oblige him', upon which he had taken out a number of £5 notes, some wrapped in brown paper. It seems he had asked her daughter, Grace, to guess how much money was there, and she had guessed £1,000, but he told her there was actually nearly £2,000, the result of a 'good business deal'. Young had returned the next morning for the money, saying he had decided to put it in the bank, and he came back early on Wednesday to collect the car, a small black Ford saloon, claiming to have 'an early appointment'. He left around 7.15am and the car was eventually returned to Mrs Watmough by the police several weeks later.

Young's landlady, Mrs Kathleen Orford, gave evidence that Young had been staying at her lodging house in Ilford for twelve years. He had brought a man home 'for a cup of tea' on Monday 4 June and introduced him as Mr Lucas. On 6 June he had gone out early and got back just after two o'clock, and he had gone out as usual the next day but she had not seen him again, although he had telephoned a few times.

Further evidence was provided by Inspector George Smith of the Metropolitan Police, the officer who had found Young lying in the back garden of his sister's Barking address on 8 June just after midday. Young's wrists were bandaged and he was semi-conscious, and he was taken to hospital by ambulance in the company of PC Barr soon afterwards.

After a further adjournment, proceedings continued, with Mr H.H. Burrows again presiding. The next witness called was Thomas Knight, the manager of Barclays Bank in East Ham. He knew Young better than his partner, Mr Moore, because Young handled the financial side of the business, although cheques needed two signatures. On 7 June Young had paid in £500 in £5 notes to the business account, indicating that a man – named as Mr Street – was investing in the business. Young had a separate private account at the same bank, which he had only recently opened.

Then Dr Hedayatollah, senior casualty officer at Oldchurch County Hospital, Romford, confirmed that Young had been admitted to his department at around 1.30pm on 8 June. He had one wound on the right wrist and three on the left, each several inches long, together with several abrasions. The wounds could have been self-inflicted by a pocket knife.

The Lucases' milkman, Bert Dowling of Howard's Dairies, had delivered milk to the bungalow as usual on the morning of 6 June at around 9.30. He had seen the dog and heard someone moving around inside the bungalow. He had left the milk on the step without knocking.

The postman, Richard French of Lymington Avenue, Leigh, had called at the bungalow for the first time around 10am with a registered parcel for Mr Lucas. He had not seen or heard the dog, or any signs of life, but he had seen a small black saloon parked outside the gate. It was unoccupied. When he tried to deliver the package again with his final delivery of the day, around 6.30pm, the door was open and he then saw Miss Lucas returning down the steps from street level. At her request, he accompanied her into the premises where he saw the bodies of Mr and Mrs Lucas.

Giving her evidence, widow Mrs Alice Stephens, of Sunnybank, Undercliff Gardens (next door to the Lucases' bungalow), stated that Young had knocked at her door around 10 on the morning of 6 June. He asked if she knew where Mr and Mrs Lucas were as he had arrived late for a 9.30 appointment, having broken down en route, and there had been no reply from their house. As she replied in the negative, he told her to tell them that Mr James had called and that he would return later, during the evening. She heard the dog barking shortly afterwards, and saw Young standing by the back door, but had heard and seen nothing after that.

Young's sister, Mrs Joan Weeder of Barking, Essex, told the court that her brother called on her in the early afternoon of 7 June, and talked about a big business deal coming off. He gave her to understand that she would benefit from this deal, and he stayed the night because he said he had had a row with his landlady. She thought he had seemed worried, and he had complained of a headache and sore throat. Mrs Weeder had given him some tablets and he went upstairs to read, seeming much more cheerful by 8.30 that evening when she accompanied him to a call box where he made a call, giving his name for some reason as James. She didn't know who was on the other end of the telephone, and the only other part of the conversation she could recall was his saying 'I mislaid your phone number, but Mr Young gave it to me'. He seemed restless, and was happy to take more tablets before bedding down in her kitchen with her brother-in-law, another relative with nowhere to go. When she saw him next morning, he was behaving in a 'queer' way, and his wrists were bandaged, which he explained was the result of cuts from the fence in the back alley. Young said he was going to see his own doctor and went upstairs – but soon afterwards her brother-in-law called down to her because he could smell gas coming from the back bedroom. It wasn't long before the police arrived and took him away in an ambulance.

The brother-in-law, Arthur Weeder, a repatriated prisoner-of-war, said he had found Young lying on the floor in the back bedroom around noon, with a broken gas pipe in his mouth. The pipe had been broken from the wall and was 'practically in half'. Mr Weeder removed the pipe from his mouth and took Young into the garden. When lifting Young, he had seen a small knife beneath him, which belonged to the witness. The police arrived very soon after. Mr Weeder confirmed that Young's wrists were bandaged 'with handkerchiefs' and also stated that he had found a bundle of fifty one-pound notes in the wardrobe after the police had gone.

At the continuation of the hearing on 30 July the headlines in the *Southend Standard* screamed 'SENSATIONAL EVIDENCE IN MURDER TRIAL'. This was a reference to the statement that Young had made to Chief Inspector Philpott on 9 June, which the defence had evidently been trying to suppress. It seems that the sensation was not in Young's admitted dealings with Mr Lucas to profit by selling golden sovereigns, but in the details of how he had indeed killed Mr and Mrs Lucas. These details, read out by Mr Parham, the prosecuting counsel, upset young Eva Lucas so much that she fled sobbing from the court.

Young had confessed that, after an argument over the sovereigns, Mr Lucas had accused him of being a 'twister', threatened him with the police and grabbed him. This had made Young 'see red' and he 'went mad'. Admitting that he did not realise his own strength, Young had thrown Lucas across the room, picked up a chair and 'kept hitting him' with it, behaving as if 'absolutely crazy'. He then heard Mrs Lucas coming into the room and had lashed out at her several times, something that had horrified him when he realised what he had done, even though he was still 'mad' afterwards.

His statement went on to give an account of how he had taken a roll of banknotes that he saw sticking out of Mr Lucas's trouser pocket, and had taken a pouch of gems, some watches and a gold cigarette case from the roll-top desk. He put the haul down again and went out to the car, but then thought he would 'like to be seen' and so knocked next door with the intention of showing the neighbour what he had done, but he 'didn't have the heart' to upset the 'dear old lady' who answered the door so had made an excuse about looking for the Lucases. He then headed back towards Ilford, 'tortured with the terrible thought' of what he had done. Remembering the dog, he decided to go back, hoping he wouldn't 'have to kill it'. Seeing the cash and jewellery where he had left them, he decided to make it look like a robbery, and picked it all up again. No longer behaving rationally, he then took the dog, who was lying by the gate, back to Ilford with him, feeding it with sandwiches on the way. Realising later rather than sooner that he could hardly take the dog home, he dropped it off where it was likely to be found, and went back to his office to hide the jewellery before going home.

Not surprisingly, he had been unable to settle, unable to sleep and unable to decide what to do or where to go, finally settling on visiting his sister the next morning. He lied to her about a row with his landlady, and she agreed to leave him on his own in the house for a while 'to be quiet and alone', which was what he wanted, having decided to kill himself. But she came back before he had made any progress in this regard. So he spent a night on the kitchen floor with Arthur Weeder – or, as it turned out, only part of the night. After Weeder was asleep, Young first of all tried stuffing clothes up the chimney of the only empty room in the house and turning on the gas, but it seemed to have insufficient pressure. He then moved into the kitchen, putting his head on a pillow in the oven and turning on the gas, hoping that it wouldn't affect his brother-in-law. This activity, which he admitted was the behaviour of a desperate man, woke up Weeder, who told him to pull himself together and offered to try to help him sort himself out. Young turned down his offer of help and went out, saying he was going for a stroll, but instead he took a razor and a knife with him to the nearest Anderson shelter, where he slashed his wrists. But by the time daylight broke the only result was that he had lost a lot of blood, so he returned to his sister's home, intending to have another attempt when they had all gone out – but by noon he couldn't wait any longer and had accordingly broken the gas pipe, the last thing he could remember.

Another less sensational statement explained how he had divided the money he had taken between his business and his personal account. He had also bought a small car for £1,350, feeling sure he could sell it at a good profit. One last statement, given at Southend Central police station on 9 June, revealed that Young had taken the Lucases' post with him when he had left the bodies behind, and opened it. As a result he had phoned Mr Banks, a solicitor who had written to Mr Lucas requesting a visit, explaining that Mr Lucas was 'indisposed', and had then phoned Mr Lucas's office, saying he was Mr Banks, to be told that Mr Lucas was dead. Odder and odder.

In addition to the statements, Detective Sergeant David Hislop of New Scotland Yard produced some tangible evidence in court – pieces of the chair and other furniture, for example, and blood-stained clothing belonging to Mr Lucas. This witness had been in the company of Chief Inspector Philpott, among others, when they visited Young at Oldchurch Hospital on 9 June. When Philpott told Young that they were investigating the murders of Mr and Mrs Lucas, Young had said: 'I've been expecting you. It was me.'

Mr Flint now contended that these statements were inadmissible because of the state Young was in at this point, and insisted that no caution had been given to his client before his first statement was made. Elaborating his point, Mr Flint denied the usefulness of a statement made when the defendant had just attempted suicide, had lost a lot of blood, had been brought round 'quite rudely' after gas poisoning, had had his wrists stitched up, had eaten little food, had little sleep and been forced to wear clothes stiff with blood before being taken in a police car to the police station in the company of 'burly' police officers just minutes earlier.

Mr Burrows, the Chairman, after some consultation, felt that the statements were acceptable, however. On the final day of the hearing, there was little to add to what had gone before. Chief Inspector Philpott showed the shoe and the clothing he had retrieved from Mrs Weeder's home. These had been examined by Dr Davison of the police laboratory in Hendon. Mr Parham from the DPP also handed in statutory declarations of scientific evidence. Young was formally charged and cautioned, with Mr Flint recommending he plead not guilty at the October Essex Assizes.

To support his 'not guilty' plea, Young subsequently gave an account of how, as a teenager, he had been knocked down by a tramcar in Cardiff, sustaining head injuries, and had suffered a further head injury at school. Additionally, the defence – Messrs Eddy and Simmons – had managed to trace a total of four close relatives who had mental health problems. However, in spite of Young's claims of 'temporary insanity', declaring that a 'demon entered into him', this defence did not save him. Dr Lyster, the Medical Officer of Chelmsford prison, and Dr Grierson, the Senior Medical Officer of Brixton prison (who had visited

Albert Pierrepoint, executioner. (*Triple Knot*)

Young), both gave evidence that there was no trace of insanity.

It transpired that Young had met Lucas when he (Young) had some rings for sale, but he had then lied about being able to get some sovereigns at a good price so that Lucas could sell them on at a profit. Lucas evidently regarded Young as honest and had handed over £600 for him to purchase these non-existent sovereigns. Young had then started to dip into the money. Having finally told Lucas that the promised sovereigns were a myth, he had not been surprised at the anger of his reaction. 'We struggled and I struck him again and again. Hearing a noise . . . I saw a woman . . . I struck blindly. I felt as if I was striking an army.' Lucas was relieved at this stage to have come to the end of six months of 'mental agony'.

The jury, after an hour's retirement, returned a verdict of guilty. Young listened to the sentence of death, and said 'Thank you, sir' before smiling at the court and being taken out. Having lost his appeal, not unexpectedly, Young was executed on Friday 21 December at 8am by Albert Pierrepoint at Pentonville prison.

# CHAPTER 22

# Jealousy in Thorpe Bay

RAF men and airborne troops packed the court room when 27-year-old Sergeant James McNicol, originally from Motherwell, was charged with murdering another sergeant, Donald Kirkaldie, in a Nissen hut at the AA gunsite on St Augustine's Avenue on 17 August 1945. McNicol was also charged with shooting and attempting to murder Sergeant Leonard Cox at the same time and place.

The headlines in the *Southend Standard* of 21 September emphasised the potential 'Jealousy Motive' following a quarrel between the men over an ATS girl, 23-year-old brunette Jean Neale.

McNicol entered court in his uniform, his fair hair combed sleekly back. His defence was to be handled by Mr J.P. Nolan, the prosecution by Mr J.F. Claxton. The latter opened the trial, explaining that McNicol, Cox and Neale had all arrived in Southend in June, having served for differing periods of time elsewhere.

Filling in the background, Mr Claxton explained that on 6 August McNicol had been put in charge of a PT course at Rochford. This position seems to have entitled him to a rifle, but not to ammunition. It appears that the Thorpe Bay site had a small arms and ammunition store, the key of which was kept in the front office for any sergeant to access. Oddly, this key seemed to fit several locks. The stores were searched after the shootings and a long Lee Enfield rifle was found to be missing; it was subsequently located in a field at some distance from the gunsite.

Mr Claxton then moved on to the motive in the case. Private Jean Evelyn Neale had befriended Cox before McNicol arrived on the scene. She met the latter at the Halfway House public house on the seafront and they had a few dates during August, joining in the premature VJ day celebrations at the camp on 14

August, after which they had parted company at 4.30am the next morning. However, it seems that the next day Neale had declined another late night and they had quarrelled.

A full-blooded celebration took place at the camp on VJ-plus-one day (16 August), complete with dancing and a bonfire. Cox invited McNicol, with whom he was reasonably friendly, to the Halfway House where they downed five pints of beer each, and then clubbed together to buy a further six quarts of beer to take back to the camp. They returned to drink in the sergeants' mess, but Neale and another RAF man, Jerry Mackay, left to attend a dance in the NAAFI building. McNicol followed them and, when they paused to let him pass, threw beer over them both. Private Neale called to Sergeant Cox, who remonstrated with McNicol and asked him why he had done it. The answer was: 'I don't like him and I don't like you. I never have done.' At this point they were pulled apart by bystanders before the quarrel could develop further.

However, the quarrels continued at intervals during the course of the evening. When Cox returned to his Nissen hut at around 12.30, he found his bed had been turned over. Apparently McNicol had admitted doing this earlier. It was Kirkaldie who decided to tie a rope between the door and their beds so they would know if anyone entered after they had settled down to sleep, it being around 1am.

They were awoken by the rope being tugged, but that was immediately followed by the sound of the window being smashed, and the light was turned on, leaving Cox, who had

Thorpe Bay beach in the 1940s, close to the murder scene. (*Author's Collection*)

jumped out of bed, in full view of anyone outside. He saw a movement, heard a report, felt a blow and fell, shot in the chest. Shortly afterwards he heard a second shot, the one that killed Kirkaldie. In the meantime the other sergeants in the hut had obviously been roused, and pandemonium now reigned. Some of the men tried to help Cox, although it was clear they could do nothing for Kirkaldie. In the meantime McNicol had made his escape. He was spotted by a police war reserve constable shortly afterwards walking along the seafront without his boots, but his explanation, that someone had stolen his boots at the celebrations, satisfied the constable concerned. An hour and a half later – at 5.40am – he was found, asleep and fully dressed, at another gunsite at Butlers Farm, Rochford, by Inspector Hemson, who had gone there to find him after being called out to attend the scene of the shooting.

McNicol was cautioned, and taken to Southend Central police station, seemingly sober. He was detained, and later that night was ready to make a statement. As a result, he was charged with the murder of Kirkaldie, his only response being that he 'didn't know' he had killed him. He also directed the police to the rear of the coastguard station at Thorpe Bay where they eventually found the missing Lee Enfield rifle, buried with its bolt drawn and the magazine and breech full of earth.

The prosecution felt that the motive for the shot at Cox was clear, given the events of the evening, but could not explain why Kirkaldie had also been shot. A detailed description of the injuries of the deceased was given by Dr H.P. Hiscocks, the police surgeon. Kirkaldie was a well-developed man in his late 20s. There was a jagged triangular wound on the left side of his mouth, and another on the right side, the two wounds linked by a further penetrating wound across the floor of the mouth, beneath the tongue. The lower jaw was smashed into multiple fragments, and there was a third wound at the mid-line of the neck running between the thyroid cartilage and the lower jaw. Death was probably instantaneous, the result of shock and haemorrhaging following the gunshot wound to the lower face and neck. The deceased was identified by Captain John Owen of the 494th (M) Heavy Anti-Aircraft Battery RA as Sergeant Donald Alfred Richard Kirkaldie RA, aged 27, a married man with one child whose home address was in Ramsgate. The case was adjourned for a few days at this juncture.

Cox was the first to give evidence when the murder trial resumed. He said that, when he had discovered his overturned bed, with the blankets thrown about, he had asked McNicol if it was his idea of a joke. The accused suggested that they settle the matter in the boxing ring outside but Cox did not trust him in the dark and McNicol did not want to fight in the hut, so he went to the sergeants' mess to continue drinking.

The man who had been soaked in beer, LAC Gerald Mackay, who lived at Fermoy Road, Thorpe Bay, said he was invited to the Victory Dance at the gunsite and had no idea why he had been targeted. When Mackay had wiped the beer out of his eyes he saw McNicol standing there with an empty pint glass; he said: 'I threw it. Do you want to make something of it?' It was at this point that Cox intervened.

After a further adjournment Private Jean Neale gave her evidence. She had been out with McNicol four times during August, the last time being the night before VJ day. On Wednesday 13 August she had joined him for something to eat around 10.30pm, and they had headed towards the seafront before changing their minds. McNicol had kept her talking by the ATS billets but Neale had wanted to go into the hut. Finally he had thrown her bag on the floor and said 'Well, go back to the hut' and she told him 'That's the last of you' and went inside.

Neale had gone to the dance on 16 August with her friend Private 'Ginger' Searle, another ATS, and they had met up with Cox and Mackay. After a few dances, she and Mackay had been standing in the porch when McNicol approached, with another two sergeants, and threw the beer over them. He 'seemed to have had rather a lot of drink'.

Inspector Hemson related how he had been called to the camp at 3.45am on 17 August and found the body of a soldier in a bed with wounds to his throat. On the floor was Sergeant Cox with a wound in his chest. There were two broken window panes and a bullet hole in the wall. At 5am he started to search for McNicol and went with other officers to the gunsite at Butler's Farm, Shopland. McNicol was lying on a bed in the sergeants' hut, seemingly asleep. Hemson had woken him by lifting his wrist, and then asked for his name, after which he was taken to the mess room and searched. According to the inspector, he appeared 'to be in a normal condition'.

Later the same day Inspector Hemson saw McNicol again, with Detective Inspector Harris, at which point McNicol made a statement. He described how he had been drinking at the Halfway House until it closed, and had then seen Neale at the camp bonfire and told her he would probably see her at the dance. He had returned for a few drinks at the bar and saw 'Jean with a civvy chap'. He had jumped to the conclusion that Mackay was her date, rather than him, and this had upset him: 'I wanted to know whether she was going with me or the civvy.' Having taken a pint of beer to drink in the dance hall, he saw them again, and was unhappy at the thought of her 'going with a civvy man while I was in the Forces', so he had tipped his beer over Mackay. After a bit of a struggle Cox had come running over, 'taking the civvy's part', so McNicol had wanted to fight him too, but the people around had stopped him.

McNicol claimed that not long after this Cox had pushed him against some chairs and tables outside the dance hall and tried to fight him then and there, but McNicol asked him to move away from the vicinity of the dance hall. Then the prisoner had returned to the bar until the dance was finished. Cox and Kirkaldie had later come into the mess where McNicol, still drinking beer, had been addressed by Cox, using obscene language and saying something about killing him 'if he hadn't another three weeks to do in the Army'. Left alone to think things over, McNicol had not wanted to appear afraid of Cox and decided to 'really have a good hit at him'. He walked around the camp, thinking about Cox's claim that he would kill him, and wondering how best to avoid being beaten up by Cox, until he 'found himself' in the Command Post where he was able to help himself to a rifle.

Claiming that he had no intention of killing Cox but only wanted to wound him, McNicol went to his quarters, broke the window and switched on the light. He could see Cox and 'about six men' and, feeling unable to 'draw back' at this stage, he tried to shoot Cox in the leg, firing two or three times. Although he knew he was doing wrong, his statement professed that he didn't know what else to do. So he walked to the Rochford gunsite and lay on his bed, knowing that the police would come, but seemingly unaware that he had killed Sergeant Kirkaldie.

The final stage in this case took place at the Chelmsford Assizes in November, with Mr Cecil Havers KC opening for the prosecution, quoting the statement that McNicol had made to the police. Mr Tristram Beresford, defending, asked Jean Neale if McNicol should have been jealous of either Cox or Kirkaldie, but she knew of no reason why that should be suggested. Beresford's suggestion was that the jury should bring in a verdict of manslaughter on the grounds that McNicol was too drunk to form any intention of killing anyone, his intoxication exacerbated by malaria medication.

McNicol, in his last chance to give evidence, admitted that he had taken a short bayonet from his kitbag after the beer throwing, and kept it in his pocket 'in case' he needed it against Cox. This he had fixed on to the rifle which he later removed from the unlocked armoury along with five rounds. But yet again, when questioned by Beresford, he said that this was done to defend himself and to frighten Cox, not to kill him or Kirkaldie.

Two sergeants, Thompson and Abley, then gave evidence that McNicol was not, in their opinion, drunk on the evening in question. However, the war reserve constable PC Mead, who had seen McNicol without his boots on the seafront after the incident, was not so convinced of his sobriety at this point. It seems that McNicol had thrown the boots over a hedge after he had buried the rifle and cleaned up his face and hands in the sea – but he could not explain why he had done any of these things.

Under cross-examination by Mr Havers, McNicol said he had switched on the light so he could hit Cox 'in a dangerous spot'. He also said he had fired blindly into the hut to 'scare the others', without thinking he might actually hit someone.

The jury took just an hour to return a verdict of guilty, and McNicol, described by the *Southend Standard* as a 'short, sturdy figure in uniform', stood stiffly to attention while Mr Justice Lewis passed sentence of death. Saying 'Thank you, my Lord' in firm tones, McNicol turned smartly and ran down the dock steps to the cells below.

McNicol's appeal was rejected on 19 December even though a petition for his reprieve had been signed by 20,000 people. He was executed on the morning of Friday 21 December by Albert Pierrepoint at Pentonville prison in London, just an hour and a half after John Young. It was a sad end to the post-war celebrations.

Albert Pierrepoint, incidentally, was a professional executioner who was responsible for more than 450 official deaths, including the last two detailed above, and was the last in a family of professional executioners. Yet he was subsequently to denounce the death penalty as a deterrent and became a confirmed abolitionist. In his autobiography, he wrote that 'I do not now believe that any one of the hundreds of executions I carried out has in any way acted as a deterrent against future murder. Capital punishment, in my view, achieved nothing except revenge.'

# Bibliography

Beck, Maurice, *Policing before Police Forces* (Essex Police Museum, no date)

Benham, Hervey, *The Smugglers Century* (Essex Records Office, no. 94, 1986)

Benton, Philip, *A History of Rochford Hundred* (A. Harrington, 1867)

*Calendar of Assize Records Essex Indictments: Elizabeth I* (HMSO, 1978)

*Calendar of Assize Records Essex Indictments: James I* (HMSO, 1982)

Chisman, Norman M., *Bygone Benfleet* (Phillimore & Co., Chichester, 1991)

Church, Robert, *Murder in East Anglia* (Robert Hale, London, 1987)

Cloud, Yvonne (ed.), *Beside the Seaside* (Stanley Nott, London, 1934)

Cockburn, J.S. (ed.), *Crime in England, 1550–1800* (Methuen, London, 1977)

Day, J.W., *The James Wentworth Day Book of Essex* (Egon Publishers, Letchworth, 1979)

Deary, Terry, *The Measly Middle Ages* (Scholastic, London, 1996)

Denney, Patrick, *Foul Deeds and Suspicious Deaths in and around Colchester* (Wharncliffe Books, Barnsley, 2005)

Emmison, F.G., *Elizabethan Life: disorder* (Essex County

Council, 1970)

Evans, Stewart P., *Executioner: the Chronicles of a Victorian Hangman* (Sutton Publishing, Stroud, 2004)

Gardiner, Tom, *Broomstick over Essex and East Anglia* (Ian Henry Publications, Romford, 1981)

Goodman, Anthony, *The Loyal Conspiracy* (Routledge & Kegan Paul, London, 1971)

Gordon, Dee, *People who Mattered in Southend and Beyond* (Ian Henry Publications, Romford, 2006)

Gray, Adrian, *Crime and Criminals in Victorian Essex* (Countryside Books, Newbury, 1988)

Greenblatt, Stephen (ed.), *The Norton Shakespeare: Richard II* (Norton & Co., London, 1997)

Grieve, Hilda, *The Sleepers and the Shadows* vol. 1 (Essex Record Office, 1988)

Guy, John, *Medieval Life* (Entertainment Ltd, 2003)

Hill, Marion, *The Honeypot Killers* (Next Century Books, Beds, 2000)

Hill, Tony, *Guns and Gunners at Shoeburyness* (Baron Books, Buckingham, 1999)

*History of Prittlewell Priory* (Southend Museum Publication no. 4, 1922)

*Hutchinson Illustrated Encyclopedia of British History* (Helicon Publishing, Oxford, 1995)

Jarvis, Stan, *Essex Pride* (Ian Henry Publications, Romford, 1984)

Jarvis, Stan, *Smuggling in East Anglia, 1700–1840* (Countryside Books, Newbury, 1987)

Jarvis, Stan, *Essex Murder Casebook* (Countryside Books, Newbury, 1994)

Johnson, W.H., *Essex Tales of Mystery and Murder* (Countryside Books, Newbury, 2001)

Johnson, W.H., *Essex Villains* (Countryside Books, Newbury, 2004)

Keeble, N.H., *Richard II by William Shakespeare York Notes (Advanced)* (York Press, London, 1988)

Knights, Edward S., *Essex Folk* (Heath Cranton Ltd, London, 1935)

Latham, Robert, *The Shorter Pepys* (Bell & Hyman Ltd, London, 1986)

Lewis, Geoffrey, *Behind the Walls* (Ian Henry Publications, Romford, 1996)

Liddell, W.H. and Wood, R.G. (eds), *Essex and the Peasants' Revolt* (Essex Record Office, no. 81, 1981)

Liddell, W.H. and Wood, R.G. (eds), *Essex and the Great Revolt of 1381* (Essex Record Office, 1984)

Maple, Eric, *The Dark World of Witches* (Robert Hale, London, 1962)

Morgan, Glyn, *Secret Essex* (Ian Henry Publications, Romford, 1982)

Neale, Kenneth, *Essex in History* (Phillimore & Co., Chichester, 1977)

Nichols, J.F., *Southchurch Hall* (The Public Library & Museum Committee Corporation, 1932)

Occomore, D., *Curiosities of Essex* (Ian Henry Publications, Romford, 1984)

Orford, Maureen, *The Shoebury Story* (Ian Henry Publications, Romford, 2000)

Payne, Jessie, K., *Southend on Sea, A Pictorial History* (Phillimore & Co., Chichester, 1985)

Payne, Jessie K., *Ghost Hunter's Guide to Essex* (Ian Henry Publications, Romford, 1987)

Pearce, Marion, *Milton, Chalkwell and the Crowstone* (Ian Henry Publications, Romford, 2000)

Pierrepoint, Albert, *Executioner: Pierrepoint* (Geo. Harrap &

Co. Ltd, London, 1974)

Pool, Daniel, *What Jane Austen Ate and Charles Dickens Knew* (Robinson Publishing, London, 1998)

Priestley, Harold, *Essex Crime and Criminals* (Ian Henry Publications, Romford, 1986)

Priestley, H.E. and Phillips, W.T., *A History of Benfleet* (Castle Point District Council, 1977)

Roe, Fred, *Essex Survivals* (Methuen, London, 1929)

Samaha, Joel, *Law and Order in Historical Perspective* (Academic Press, New York, 1974)

Saul, Nigel, *Richard II* (Yale University Press, 1997)

Sharpe, J.A., *Crime in Seventeenth-Century England* (The Press Syndicate, Cambridge, 1983)

Sipple, Mavis, *Titbits and Tales of Essex Inns* (Brent Publications, 2001)

Sipple, Mavis, *Rochford, A History* (Phillimore & Co., Chichester, 2004)

Smith, Ken, *Canewdon: a pattern of life through the ages* (Ian Henry Publications, Romford, 1987)

Storey, Neil R., *Grim Almanac of Essex* (Sutton Publishing, Stroud, 2005)

Stratmann, Linda, *Essex Murders* (Sutton Publishing, Stroud, 2004)

Torry, J.G., *Chelmsford Prison* (East Anglian Magazine Ltd, Ipswich, 1980)

Totterdell, G.H., *Country Copper* (Geo. Harrap, London, 1956)

Trevelyan, G.M., *English Social History* (Pelican Books, 1967)

Vingoe, Lesley, *Hockley, Hullbridge and Hawkwell Past* (Phillimore & Co., Chichester, 1999)

Ward, Jennifer C., *The Essex Gentry & the County Community in the Fourteenth Century* (Essex Record Office, 1991)

Williams, Judith, *Leigh-on-Sea: A History* (Phillimore & Co.,

Chichester, 2002)

Williams, Judith, *Shoeburyness, A History* (Phillimore & Co., Chichester, 2006)

Williams, Judith, *Wickford: A History* (Phillimore & Co., Chichester, 2006)

Winn, Christopher, *I Never Knew that About England* (Ebury Publishing, London, 2003)

Yearsley, Ian, *Islands of Essex* (Ian Henry Publications, Romford, 1994)

Yearsley, Ian, *Hadleigh Past* (Phillimore & Co., Chichester, 1998)

Yearsley, Ian, *Essex Events* (Phillimore & Co., Chichester, 1999)

Yearsley, Ian, *A History of Southend* (Phillimore & Co., Chichester, 2001)

## Magazines, Newspapers and Journals

Too numerous to mention, but including copies of *Essex Review, The Times, Essex Countryside* and *Southend Standard* at Southend Central Library, *Chelmsford Chronicle* at Essex Record Office, and *Illustrated Police News* and *Essex Weekly News* at the British Library, Colindale.

# Index